Wise Women

of the Bible

By Karajah Yashar

PASSED OVER PRESS

TRUTH BEYOND TRADITION

Orlando, FL

Wise Women
of the Bible

ISBN: 978-1-962691-59-8
First Edition: February 2026

Acknowledgements

Louise Neverson (1913-2005)

This book is for granny—the first woman who showed me, through quiet yet solid faith, what a woman of God rooted in Scripture truly looks like. May you continue to shine down from heaven, your legacy still guiding and covering us. This is also a tribute to my mother, and my sisters—the women I grew up with, learned from, and was shaped by long before I ever understood the weight of Scripture or the power of legacy. Your strength, wisdom, patience, virtue, and endurance laid a foundation in me that no classroom could ever provide. You modeled resilience, faith, and love in ways both spoken and silent, and those lessons continue to guide my life and my work.

I also honor all the wise women I have encountered along the way—teachers, elders, friends, and sisters in the faith—whose counsel, correction, encouragement, and example helped shape who I am today. This book exists because of you. Your lives, your voices, and your faithfulness are reflected in these pages. May this work stand as a small offering of gratitude, a recognition that the wisdom you carry matters, and a tribute to the role women play in building, preserving, and restoring what God has ordained.

Table of Contents

Introduction

The women of the Bible were never silent figures standing in the background of a man's story. They were thinkers, leaders, mothers, prophets, warriors, servants, and survivors. They wrestled with fear, faith, loss, courage, obedience, and hope—often in seasons that demanded more of them than comfort would allow. Their lives were not preserved in Scripture to be admired from a distance, but to be *heard*, learned from, and lived out again.

Wise Women of the Bible invites you to encounter these women not merely as historical names, but as living witnesses whose stories still carry breath and power. Here, their experiences are told as though they are speaking for themselves—out of their own lips—sharing the wisdom forged in moments of obedience, the pain born of sacrifice, and the faith required to stand when standing cost everything.

These women knew what it meant to trust God in private before being used by Him in public. They understood waiting, surrender, resilience, and holy boldness. Some were celebrated, others overlooked. Some were queens, others servants. Some were remembered for one defining moment, others for a lifetime of faithfulness. Yet each one carried a message that reaches across generations to speak directly to women today.

This book is not simply about what these women *did*, but about who they *became* through their encounters with God.

Their voices challenge modern assumptions about strength, purpose, beauty, submission, leadership, and calling. They remind us that influence is not always loud, obedience is not always easy, and faith is often proven in unseen places.

As you journey through these pages, listen closely. Their stories are mirrors, warnings, encouragements, and invitations. The women of the Bible are still speaking—and their words are meant for you.

Historical Fact: Between the years 1492-1860, 80% of the *men* taken from West Africa in the Trans-Atlantic slave trade were circumcised in the flesh. This is one of the indicators solidifying that 'Africans' taken in bondage were the lost sheep of Israel. "And ye shall circumcise the flesh of your foreskin; and it shall be a token of the covenant betwixt me and you" Genesis 17:11. Another indicator is the prophecy of Deuteronomy 28:15-68 which says the Children of Israel would be taken captive by ships and sold into bondage.

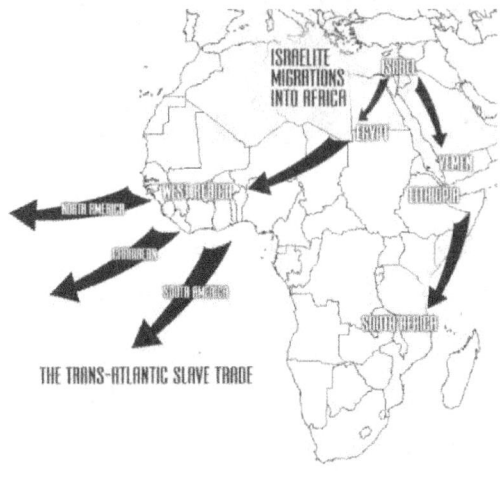

Chapter 1: Eve

Mother of All Living, First Woman, First Bride

Eve entered the world not in thunder or fire, but in intimacy. She was born from the side of man, not from his feet to be trampled, nor from his head to rule over him, but from his rib—close to the heart. The garden was already breathing when she opened her eyes. Rivers ran. Trees stretched their branches toward heaven. The air itself carried peace. Eve awoke into harmony, into belonging, into a world where nothing yet needed fixing.

Before she had a name, she had a purpose. God saw Adam's solitude and declared it *not good*. That declaration is significant, for it was the first time anything in creation was described as lacking. Eve was the answer to that lack. She was created as a helper fit for him—not a servant, not a subordinate, but a counterpart. The Hebrew idea behind her role speaks of strength alongside strength, of mutuality, of one completing what the other could not fulfill alone. Eve was designed to stand face to face with Adam, to walk beside him, to share dominion, and to steward creation together.

In those early days, Eve lived without shame. Her body was not something to hide, and her voice was not something to suppress. She walked freely with Adam, unafraid of God, unburdened by fear, untouched by self-consciousness. Their union was seamless. Scripture says they were one flesh, and in the garden, that truth was visible—not merely in marriage, but in motion, in purpose, in thought. They moved as a single harmony, a shared life expressed through two bodies.

Eve's mind was curious, her heart receptive. She named nothing, yet she perceived much. She listened. She observed. She engaged. When the serpent approached her, it was not ignorance that made her vulnerable, but a desire to understand. The serpent did not tempt her with rebellion first; he tempted her with wisdom. He questioned God's word, and in doing so, invited Eve into a conversation that felt thoughtful rather than dangerous. The lie came softly, wrapped in reason and promise. *You will not surely die. You will be like God.*

Eve stood at the crossroads of trust and autonomy. The fruit was pleasing to the eye, desirable for gaining wisdom. In that moment, she made a decision that would echo through every generation that followed. She reached. She ate. She shared. This was not an act of isolation—Adam was with her. Their unity did not dissolve in the moment of disobedience; rather, it carried them together into consequence.

The fall did not shatter their marriage immediately, but it fractured their innocence. Their eyes were opened, not to enlightenment, but to exposure. Shame rushed in where peace once lived. They covered themselves, not because their bodies had changed, but because their perception had. For the first time, Eve knew fear. For the first time, she hid.

After the curse, Eve's role shifted, but her significance did not diminish. God spoke directly to her, naming the sorrow that would now accompany life. Childbearing would bring pain. Desire would now wrestle with imbalance. The harmony she once knew would require effort, endurance, and grace. Yet even within the curse, hope was planted. God promised that her seed would bruise the serpent's head. Eve, the one through whom sin entered the world, would also become the channel through which redemption would come.

It is after the fall that Adam names her Eve—*the mother of all living*. This naming is not incidental. It is prophetic. Though death had entered the world, Eve's legacy would be life. She would carry humanity forward, womb by womb, generation by generation. She would bear sons in a world now marked by labor and loss. She would know joy and grief, pride and heartbreak. Cain would rise from her body, and so would Abel. One would become a murderer; the other a martyr. Eve lived long enough to understand that motherhood is both miracle and mourning.

Her marriage, too, was transformed. One flesh remained true, but now it required forgiveness. Adam blamed her. She explained herself. The simplicity of Eden was gone. Love had to mature. Partnership had to survive disappointment. Eve's life teaches that marriage does not end at failure; it is tested there. The one flesh union endured exile, toil, and tragedy. Together, they left the garden. Together, they worked the ground. Together, they buried a son. Their unity was no longer effortless, but it was real.

Eve is often remembered for her mistake, but Scripture preserves her for much more. She was the first to experience God's creative tenderness. The first to wrestle with temptation. The first to give birth. The first to suffer loss. The first woman to hope for deliverance through her children. She lived long enough to see Seth born, a replacement seed, a sign that God was still working His plan through her line.

Eve's story speaks to women today not as a warning alone, but as a witness. She reminds us that curiosity can be holy when anchored in trust, and dangerous when divorced from obedience. She shows us that mistakes do not erase calling. That motherhood is sacred even when painful. That marriage is resilient when rooted in covenant rather than perfection.

Eve was not silent in Scripture because she had nothing to say. She was foundational because everything that followed stood on her beginning. From her came nations, prophets, kings, and finally, the Messiah. Her life is a reminder that the first woman was not created to fall—but even when she did, God wove her failure into a story of redemption.

Eve still speaks. She speaks of beginnings and consequences, of unity and fracture, of sorrow and hope. She speaks as the mother of all living, as the first bride, as a woman whose life reminds us that even after exile, God continues to walk with humanity—just outside the garden gate.

A Message from Eve

I have watched the world grow loud. I have watched women forget the sound of their own breath, forget the wisdom of their own bodies, forget the tenderness they were born carrying. I speak now not as a myth, not as a warning carved in stone, but as a woman who lived, who chose, who learned, and who endured.

Do not be fooled by the world's voice. It still sounds like the serpent—smooth, reasonable, persuasive. It still questions what God has said without ever denying Him outright. It still tells you that you are lacking, that you need more, that obedience is ignorance and restraint is weakness. I believed that once. I learned that wisdom stolen is never the same as wisdom given. What God gives freely does not come with shame hidden inside it.

Do not have shame in your body. Before fear entered me, before guilt learned my name, my body was good. It was God's idea before it was ever judged by man. I walked uncovered and unafraid. My skin did not apologize for itself. My form did not need permission to exist. Shame was not born in the body—it was born in disobedience. Do not confuse the two. Your body is not the mistake. Your body is not the curse. Your body is still capable of life, pleasure, nurture, and praise.

Eat of the trees God gave you. Not the ones the world advertises with glitter and urgency, but the ones planted by His own hand—trees of nourishment, truth, patience, rest, and joy. God is not stingy. Eden was full. I forgot that. I let one forbidden thing make me overlook abundance. Do not starve yourself chasing what was never meant to sustain you.

Always be on guard against the serpent. He does not arrive announcing danger. He arrives asking questions that sound thoughtful, affirming doubts that feel intellectual, validating feelings that slowly unmoor you from truth. He does not rush you—he waits. Be watchful. Stay rooted. Conversations matter. What you entertain in your mind will eventually reach your hands.

Let your desire be to your own husband—singular, focused, protected. I learned that unity is fragile when desire wanders. One flesh is not merely a bond of bodies, but of attention, loyalty, and intention. Guard your covenant. What is scattered loses strength. What is focused becomes powerful.

And hear this clearly: learn from my mistake, but do not let it define you. I fell—and I still became the mother of all living. I failed—and God still trusted my womb with the future. Redemption did not erase my past, but it redeemed my purpose. You, too, can write a redemption story. You are not disqualified by what you reached for too soon, trusted too easily, or believed too deeply without wisdom.

I am Eve. I was first, but I was not finished by failure. Neither are you.

Lessons I will Take from Eve

_____

_____

_____

_____

_____

_____

_____

_____

_____

Chapter 2: Sarah

The Woman Who Carried Promise
Through Waiting

Sarah's story does not begin with motherhood. It begins with movement. With leaving. With a woman packing up a life she already knew and stepping into a future she could not yet explain.

When she is first introduced in Scripture, she is beautiful and she is barren—two words that the world has always tried to turn into a verdict. Beauty, as if it is her value. Barrenness, as if it is her shame. But Sarah is neither ornament nor tragedy. She is the first matriarch of a covenant line, a woman whose life proves that promise can live inside delay, and that God can write purpose through seasons that feel like silence.

She is Sarai then, before the name is widened into Sarah, "princess," before her identity becomes a banner that future generations will inherit. Sarai is a wife, a companion, a witness to a call that does not start with her lips but will shape her whole body. Her husband, Abram, hears God speak—Leave your country, your kindred, your father's house—and Sarai goes with him. That "with him" matters. People love to tell the story as if Abram walked in faith and Sarai simply followed behind like a shadow. But a woman does not leave everything familiar without a faith of her own. A woman does not trade stability for a tent without believing something deeper than comfort is at work.

So she goes.

She learns the dust of long roads. The thin sleep of unfamiliar places. The ache of always being a stranger. She learns what it means to be the quiet strength behind a man who is learning to become a nation before he ever becomes a father. She learns how to be supportive without being invisible, present without being powerless.

Sarah and Abraham

One Flesh, Two People Learning Covenant

Sarah's marriage to Abraham is not a fragile love story. It is a covenant partnership tested by fear, stretched by waiting, and refined through conflict. Their "one flesh" is not the soft kind of unity that survives only in easy seasons. It is the unity that holds even when the world presses in.

Twice, Abraham—trying to protect himself—introduces Sarah as his sister. It is one of the most uncomfortable truths in the narrative: the man of promise still carries fear in his bones. And Sarah, the wife of promise, becomes vulnerable because of it. Her beauty draws attention, and the danger of that attention is real. Sarah is caught in the consequences of Abraham's decisions, yet she is also preserved by God's intervention. The story quietly reveals something women still know too well: sometimes a woman's life is made fragile by the choices of the one who is supposed to cover her.

But Sarah does not live in bitterness as her defining language. She continues to walk with Abraham. Continues to build a life in motion. Continues to host guests and manage tents and endure the private grief of a womb that will not open.

And still—God does not remove her from the promise because her husband was imperfect. God does not replace her because her season is long. The covenant keeps moving forward, and Sarah is still in it.

The Weight of Waiting

When Time Feels Like a Closed Door

Years pass, and what begins as patience starts to feel like humiliation. Sarah has a front-row seat to her own unanswered prayer. People can pretend that faith makes waiting painless, but Sarah's story refuses that lie. Waiting can be holy and still be heavy.

The promise is spoken: descendants, land, a future. Yet Sarah's body tells a different story every month. It tells her, *Not yet. Not this time. Still empty.*

And this is where Sarah becomes deeply human, deeply relatable, and deeply instructive.

Because Sarah makes a decision.

She does what many do when delay becomes unbearable: she tries to help God.

She offers Hagar to Abraham as a surrogate, thinking perhaps the promise can come through another woman's womb. It is not a petty decision. It is a desperate one. It is a decision born from cultural pressure, personal grief, and the fear that she will be the reason the promise fails. Sarah is trying to survive the emotional tension between what God said and what life seems to be saying louder.

Hagar conceives, and the atmosphere in the tent changes. Pregnancy is not just biology—it is status. It shifts the power dynamic. It creates pride in one and pain in another. Scripture records that Hagar begins to despise Sarah, and Sarah feels it, carries it, cannot ignore it. Now she is not only barren; she is surrounded by evidence of fruitfulness that is not hers.

Sarah responds with intensity. Some will call it cruelty. Some will call it jealousy. It is complicated, as most real-life family conflicts are. But it is also important to say this: the Bible does not present Sarah as a cartoon villain or a perfect saint. It shows her as a woman with authority in her house and sorrow in her soul.

Her decision creates consequences that ripple far beyond her lifetime. Yet even here, God shows that He sees everyone in the story—Sarah, Hagar, Ishmael—without denying covenant order or ignoring human pain.

Humility and Honor

"Calling Abraham Lord"

Sarah's humility is not weakness. It is structured strength.

In later Scripture, Sarah is held up as an example of a wife who honored her husband, "calling him lord." That line is often misunderstood, and it can be weaponized by people who want women silent, small, and afraid. But in Sarah's story, honor is not presented as humiliation; it is presented as a posture.

Sarah's honor is the kind that recognizes covenant headship without erasing her own voice. Because Sarah is not voiceless.

She speaks. She challenges. She makes plans. She insists. She laughs out loud. She negotiates emotional realities inside a marriage that includes real tension.

Calling Abraham "lord" is not Sarah saying, "I am nothing." It is Sarah demonstrating a reverence for the covenant structure of her household. It is respect that does not require the disappearance of her personhood. She is not reduced in the text—she is remembered.

And it is striking that God Himself reinforces Sarah's significance. When Abraham is uncertain about sending Hagar and Ishmael away, God tells him to listen to Sarah. Not because Sarah is always right in every emotion, but because covenant promise is being guarded in that household, and Sarah is central to it.

Sarah's humility is not passivity. It is reverence with backbone.

The Laughter That Turned Into a Name

When Promise Finally Knocks

Then comes the moment that feels almost too tender for a world so harsh: God visits, and Sarah hears the promise again—this time with timing attached.

"A son."

Not eventually. Not vaguely. Not metaphorically.

A son.

Sarah laughs, and it is not the laughter of mockery alone. It is the laughter of a woman who has learned disappointment so thoroughly that joy feels unsafe. It is the laughter of a woman whose body has been told "no" for so long that "yes" sounds like a trick.

And when God asks, "Why did Sarah laugh?" Sarah denies it. That detail is so intimate—so honest. Because sometimes when you've waited too long, you don't want God to see how tired you are. You don't want to be exposed as weary. You don't want to admit that you stopped expecting the miracle.

But God does not crush her for laughing. He corrects her gently with power: "Is anything too hard for the LORD?"

And then God does what only He can do: He opens what time closed.

Sarah conceives.

Her body becomes a testimony.

And when she gives birth, the laughter changes. It becomes celebration. It becomes prophecy in sound. Her son is named Isaac—laughter—because God turned her private ache into public joy.

Now Sarah is not only wife of promise. She is mother of promise.

And motherhood does not erase the years of pain; it redeems them. Every cry of that baby is proof that delay was not denial.

Every small hand in Sarah's older hands is a reminder that God does not forget.

Isaac's Inheritance

Protecting the Covenant Line

Isaac's inheritance is not only about property. It is about covenant identity—who will carry the promise forward, who will be named in the line that will shape a nation and ultimately point toward redemption.

Sarah understands what's at stake.

When she sees Ishmael—Hagar's son—mocking or threatening the peace of Isaac's future, Sarah responds fiercely: "Cast out this bondwoman and her son: for the son of this bondwoman shall not be heir with my son, even with Isaac."

This is one of the most emotionally charged moments in the narrative, and it demands careful handling. Sarah is not simply jealous of another child. She is guarding inheritance. She is guarding covenant. She is guarding what God specifically said would come through *her* son.

And God confirms the covenant order: Isaac is the promised heir.

That does not mean Ishmael is unloved by God. God promises to bless Ishmael too, to make a great nation from him. But the covenant line—the inheritance of promise—belongs to Isaac.

In this, Sarah becomes more than a mother. She becomes a gatekeeper of destiny.

You may not like the pain of the moment, but you cannot deny the spiritual clarity: some things cannot share inheritance. Some mixtures bring conflict. Some relationships must be ordered, not because people don't matter, but because purpose does.

Sarah's life teaches that promise requires protection, and protection sometimes costs comfort.

Sarah's Later Years

The Quiet Strength of a Matriarch

After Isaac, Sarah becomes the steady center of a household that finally has laughter in it. But her story does not end with a birth. It ends with legacy.

She lives long enough to see the promise established in her son. She becomes a living monument—proof that God can do the impossible through the overlooked, the delayed, the doubted. And when Sarah dies, Abraham mourns her deeply and publicly. He purchases a burial site—an act that is both love and symbolism. It is one of the first tangible footholds of promised land belonging to their family.

Even in death, Sarah is connected to inheritance.

She is not simply buried. She is planted in covenant ground.

Why Sarah Matters

The Message Her Life Still Speaks

Sarah matters because she embodies the tension women still live in:

- The ache between promise and reality

- The pressure to "make it happen" when waiting feels humiliating

- The complexity of marriage when faith and fear share the same tent

- The power of honor that does not erase voice

- The miracle of restoration after seasons that seemed to announce endings

Sarah is not remembered because she never struggled. She is remembered because God met her in the struggle and still brought promise through her life.

She teaches women today that you can be flawed and still chosen. You can be tired and still included. You can laugh in disbelief and still become the womb of fulfillment.

And perhaps the most startling truth of Sarah's story is this:

God did not wait for Sarah to become young again. He waited until it was clear the outcome could only be Him.

So the promise would not be confused with luck, or timing, or human strength.

It would be unmistakably God.

Sarah's legacy is not just Isaac. It is the revelation that covenant does not depend on human ability—it depends on divine faithfulness. And that makes her, truly, a mother not only of one son, but of a lineage of believers who learn, through her life, how to hope again after waiting too long.

A Message from Sarah

I speak to you as a woman who waited longer than she ever planned to. I speak as a wife who walked beside a man learning how to lead before he ever knew where the road would end. I speak as one who honored her husband not because she was small, but because she understood covenant.

Honor your husband. Not with silence that swallows your voice, and not with words that sharpen like knives. Do not cut him down in private and then expect him to stand strong in public. A man cannot rise when the one closest to him keeps reminding him of his weaknesses. I learned that reverence is not submission born of fear—it is strength expressed through respect.

I called Abraham "lord" not because I forgot who I was, but because I knew who *we* were together. My honor was not low self-esteem dressed up as obedience. It was intentional. It was spiritual. It was my way of protecting the covenant we shared.

A marriage is not sustained by dominance or competition, but by mutual recognition of order, purpose, and trust.

Understand this: honoring your husband does not erase your intelligence, your discernment, or your influence. I spoke. I made decisions. I carried weight in my household. God Himself told Abraham to listen to my voice. Honor does not mean invisibility. It means choosing to build rather than dismantle.

Strong marriages create strong families. I watched how unity creates covering, and how division invites strain. When husband and wife turn against each other, the household trembles. But when they face forward together—even imperfectly—children grow up anchored. Inheritance becomes clear. Identity becomes stable. Promise has room to breathe.

Guard your words. They shape the atmosphere of your home. A man who is honored rises into responsibility. A woman who honors does not lose power—she multiplies it. You do not strengthen yourself by weakening your husband. You strengthen your future by strengthening him.

I know what it is to struggle. I know what it is to grow weary, to grow impatient, to make decisions from pain instead of peace. Learn from me, but do not repeat every mistake I made. Waiting is not failure. Delay is not denial. And honor is never wasted, even when the season feels long.

I was not perfect, but I was chosen. I was not young, but I was fruitful. I was not silent, but I was respectful. And through covenant—messy, stretching, enduring covenant—promise came forth.

I am Sarah.
Honor does not diminish you.
It positions you.

Lessons I will Take from Sarah

_____

_____

_____

_____

_____

_____

_____

_____

_____

Chapter 3: Rebekah

The Woman Who Recognized the
Future Before It Spoke

Rebekah's story begins not in a palace or a tent of inheritance, but at a well—where daily labor meets divine interruption. She is young, strong, and unguarded by privilege. When Abraham's servant arrives in her land, carrying the weight of covenant on his journey, Rebekah does not know she is standing at the threshold of history. She only knows thirst, hospitality, and instinct. And instinct—guided by God—will mark her life again and again.

She is not chosen because of lineage alone, nor because of beauty, though Scripture later implies she possessed it. Rebekah is chosen because she *acts*. When asked for water, she does not ration kindness. She draws again and again, watering not only the man but the camels—an act requiring stamina, patience, and generosity. This is not small obedience. It is strenuous faithfulness in an ordinary moment. Before Rebekah ever becomes a matriarch, she proves she can carry responsibility without being asked twice.

When the servant asks if she will leave her family and go to a man she has never met, Rebekah answers with startling clarity: *"I will go."* No bargaining. No delay. No fear recorded. Her yes echoes Sarah's, but it carries its own boldness. Rebekah steps into destiny not dragged by tradition, but led by conviction. She leaves familiarity for promise, trusting a God she has not yet fully named—but already senses.

Rebekah and Isaac

A Marriage Formed in Quiet Strength

Rebekah's marriage to Isaac is unlike the fiery beginnings of other biblical unions. Isaac is contemplative, inward, shaped by near-sacrifice and obedience. Rebekah meets him as he meditates in the field. Their love grows gently. Scripture says Isaac *loved* Rebekah—an intentional note that speaks to affection, not merely arrangement. She becomes comfort to a man still living in the shadow of his mother Sarah's death.

But Rebekah's role as wife is not passive companionship. She enters a household with legacy in its walls and promise in its future. She learns Isaac's rhythms, his tenderness, his blind spots. Where Isaac is quiet, Rebekah is perceptive. Where Isaac is steady, Rebekah is discerning. Together they form a marriage of contrast—one flesh not because they are alike, but because they are aligned.

Rebekah's barrenness mirrors Sarah's, and again, the promise pauses long enough to test faith. Isaac prays for her, and God opens her womb. But her pregnancy is not peaceful. The children struggle within her, and Rebekah does something that reveals her spiritual intelligence: she inquires of the Lord. She does not assume. She does not endure confusion silently. She seeks understanding.

God answers her plainly. Two nations are in her womb. Two peoples divided. And—most striking—the elder shall serve the younger. Rebekah becomes the first to hear this reversal of expectation. Before either son is born, she knows God's choice. This knowledge shapes everything that follows.

Motherhood and Discernment

Seeing What Others Miss

Rebekah gives birth to twins—Esau and Jacob—two sons formed in the same womb but carrying radically different destinies. Esau emerges first, strong and impulsive, a hunter with earth on his hands and appetite in his spirit. Jacob follows, grasping Esau's heel, already reaching, already positioned for struggle and inheritance.

Isaac loves Esau, drawn to his strength and the taste of wild game. Rebekah loves Jacob, drawn not by sentiment alone but by revelation. This distinction has often been reduced to favoritism, but Scripture invites deeper reading. Rebekah's love is informed by prophecy. She is not choosing a favorite; she is aligning herself with what God already revealed.

Rebekah watches her sons grow, and she understands something Isaac does not fully grasp—or perhaps does not want to. Esau treats birthright lightly. Jacob, for all his flaws, values inheritance. Rebekah knows that covenant cannot rest on impulse. She knows promise requires stewardship.

When Isaac grows old and blind, preparing to bless Esau, Rebekah hears and understands the urgency. The moment is not merely emotional—it is historical. Blessing in this household is not a formality; it is destiny spoken aloud. Rebekah stands at a crossroads between divine revelation and patriarchal habit.

And she chooses to act.

The Decision That Changed History

Risking Reputation to Protect Promise

Rebekah's decision to help Jacob obtain the blessing is one of the most debated moments in Scripture. It is layered, uncomfortable, and deeply human. She instructs Jacob. She prepares the food. She covers him in Esau's garments and goatskins. She places herself between her son and consequence, even saying, *"Let the curse be on me."*

This is not manipulation born of ambition alone. This is a woman protecting a word God already spoke. Rebekah understands that promise can be lost not because God changes His mind, but because people refuse to align with it. She also understands cost. Her actions will fracture her household. They will send Jacob into exile. They will sever daily closeness between mother and son.

Rebekah never sees Jacob again.

That truth matters.

She helps him obtain the blessing, but she pays for it with separation. Love, in her life, is not soft. It is sacrificial. She chooses destiny over comfort, future over familiarity. And history confirms the weight of her choice: through Jacob comes Israel. Through Jacob come the tribes. Through Jacob comes the lineage that will eventually carry redemption.

Rebekah discerns God's choice not because she is deceitful, but because she is attentive. She listens—to God, to patterns, to fruit. She understands that discernment sometimes requires courage that looks controversial to those who do not hear what you hear.

Rebekah's Later Years

The Quiet Cost of Obedience

After Jacob flees, Rebekah orchestrates his protection again, sending him to her brother's house under the guise of marriage preparation. She continues to think strategically, still guarding covenant, still shielding her son from Esau's rage. But Scripture grows quiet about her after this point.

That silence is heavy.

Rebekah's story does not end with public honor or recorded farewell. It ends with influence already set in motion. She fades from the narrative, but the consequences of her faithfulness expand outward for generations. Sometimes the most pivotal women do not receive poetic endings. They receive fulfilled outcomes.

Why Rebekah Matters

The Woman Who Trusted Revelation Over Appearance

Rebekah matters because she teaches women how to discern beyond surface affection and cultural preference. She shows that motherhood includes spiritual responsibility, not just nurture. She reveals that marriage does not erase discernment, and that honoring covenant sometimes means standing firm when others hesitate.

She was hospitable before she was chosen. Brave before she was secure. Attentive before she was affirmed. She acted when silence would have been safer. She protected promise even when it cost her intimacy.

Rebekah's life speaks to women who sense God's direction before others do. To women who carry revelation quietly. To women who understand that obedience is not always applauded—but it is always remembered by God.

She was not perfect. She was decisive. And through her discernment, the future of a nation shifted.

Rebekah still speaks—through wells of service, through wombs of conflict, through decisions made in faith when the stakes are high. She reminds us that sometimes, the ones who see first must also bear the cost first.

A Message from Rebekah

I speak as a woman who learned early that destiny often arrives disguised as ordinary work. I met purpose while drawing water, not while searching for greatness. That is how God often moves—quietly, deliberately—watching how you handle what seems small before trusting you with what will shape generations.

Do not underestimate your discernment. I listened when God spoke, even when His word challenged tradition, preference, and appearance. I carried revelation before anyone else did. I felt it in my body before I saw it with my eyes. When confusion stirred within me, I did not ignore it. I asked God. And He answered. Learn this: confusion is not weakness—it is an invitation to seek clarity.

I loved my husband. I honored Isaac, even when I saw what he did not. Love does not mean blindness. Covenant does not require silence. A wife may see differently without being divisive. I did not move against my husband; I moved *for* the promise. Discernment is not rebellion when it is rooted in God's word.

I loved my son Jacob because I recognized what God had placed in him. He was not perfect. Neither was I. But I knew which seed carried the future. Learn to love beyond personality and temperament. Learn to love what God is shaping, not only what is convenient or familiar. Some people are easy to admire; others are chosen to inherit.

There will be moments when obedience costs you comfort. I made a decision that protected destiny, and it cost me closeness. I never saw Jacob again. Understand this truth without fear: obedience is not always rewarded with applause. Sometimes it is rewarded with fulfillment you will not personally enjoy—but generations will.

Do not be afraid to act when God has already spoken. Waiting when God has spoken is not faith—it is hesitation. I stepped forward when others hesitated. I accepted misunderstanding to guard covenant. If God has entrusted you with insight, steward it carefully, boldly, and prayerfully.

And remember this: service prepares you for authority. Hospitality trains your hands for leadership. Faithfulness in hidden places shapes your readiness for visible responsibility. I did not become discerning overnight. I practiced generosity long before destiny called my name.

I am Rebekah.

I learned to listen before I learned to lead.

I chose promise over preference.

And I trusted God's voice even when it required courage to follow it.

Listen.

Ask.

Act.

The future is often decided by those willing to move when revelation arrives quietly.

Lessons I will Take from Rebekah

_____

_____

_____

_____

_____

_____

_____

_____

_____

Chapter 4: Leah

The Woman God Saw When Others Did Not

Leah's story begins in the quiet ache of being second. Second in affection. Second in desire. Second in a household where love seemed to have already chosen another face. Scripture introduces her not with celebration, but with contrast—*Leah was tender-eyed, but Rachel was beautiful and well-favored.* From the very first sentence, Leah is measured against her sister, and the measurement does not appear to favor her. Yet the Bible, in its unflinching honesty, tells her story anyway—because Leah's life is not a footnote to Rachel's beauty. It is a foundation for Israel's future.

Leah grows up in her father Laban's house, learning early how survival works in a world that values appearance and advantage. She understands bargaining before romance, strategy before security. When Laban deceives Jacob on the wedding night, it is Leah who is given, not because she is chosen, but because she is *available*. That truth alone carries weight: Leah enters marriage not through affection, but through arrangement. She is a wife before she is loved, bound by covenant to a man whose heart is already elsewhere.

Jacob awakens to disappointment, and Leah awakens to reality. She is married—but unwanted. Chosen—but not preferred. Present—but unseen. And yet, Leah does not leave. She stays in the marriage that did not begin with love and tries to build a life inside a longing that is never quite satisfied.

Leah and Jacob

A Marriage of Distance and Duty

Leah's relationship with Jacob is marked by asymmetry. He works fourteen years for Rachel, but Leah is the wife who occupies his tent first. Scripture does not tell us of Jacob's affection for Leah, only his duty toward her. This absence is loud. Leah is faithful in a marriage that never truly embraces her. She shares Jacob's bed, but not his heart.

Yet Leah does not grow bitter into paralysis. She turns toward God when Jacob cannot turn toward her. Each pregnancy becomes a prayer spoken through flesh and blood. Each child becomes a sentence in Leah's long conversation with heaven.

Her first son is Reuben—*"See, a son."* Her naming reveals her hope: *Now my husband will love me.* Leah believes visibility might finally earn affection.

Her second son is Simeon—*"Heard." The Lord has heard that I am unloved.* Leah begins to understand that God hears what Jacob ignores.

Her third son is Levi—*"Joined." Now my husband will be joined to me.* She still hopes proximity will produce unity.

With each birth, Leah reaches for love through motherhood, trying to bridge emotional distance with legacy. But Jacob's heart remains with Rachel. Leah's body is fruitful, but her spirit is still searching.

Then something shifts.

Her fourth son is Judah—*"Praise."* And this time, Leah does not mention Jacob at all. She says, *Now will I praise the Lord.* This is the turning point of her life. Leah stops measuring her worth by Jacob's affection and begins anchoring it in God's recognition. Praise becomes her declaration of independence from rejection.

It is not coincidence that Judah—born from a woman who learned to praise without being loved—becomes the tribe of kings. From Judah will come David. From Judah will come the Messiah. God places redemption's lineage not in the arms of the favored wife, but in the womb of the overlooked one.

Leah and Rachel

Sisters Bound by Competition and Pain

Leah's relationship with her sister Rachel is complex, tender, and painful. They are bound by blood and divided by circumstance. Rachel has Jacob's love but no children. Leah has children but not Jacob's affection. Each sister carries what the other longs for. Their rivalry is not petty—it is desperate. It is the ache of women trying to survive in a system where worth feels scarce.

Rachel envies Leah's womb. Leah envies Rachel's beauty and favor. They trade mandrakes, negotiate nights with Jacob, and live inside a competition neither truly wins. Yet Scripture shows moments of shared endurance. They are both shaped by Laban's manipulation. Both married to the same man. Both navigating a household where comparison is constant.

Leah's pain is quieter, but no less sharp. She watches Jacob celebrate Rachel while she manages the children. She lives in the shadow of a sister who is loved easily. But Leah's endurance becomes her strength. She remains rooted, consistent, and faithful in the unseen places.

Mother of Tribes

Fruitfulness Born From Faithfulness

Leah bears six sons and a daughter. Four of those sons—Reuben, Simeon, Levi, and Judah—become foundational to the nation of Israel. Levi will produce the priesthood. Judah will produce kingship. These are not minor roles. These are spiritual and governmental pillars.

It is stunning that God entrusts such weight to the woman Scripture describes as unloved. Leah's life testifies that divine favor does not follow human preference. God does not wait for Jacob's approval to validate Leah's purpose. He blesses her openly, repeatedly, unmistakably.

Later in life, Leah is buried in the Cave of Machpelah—*with Jacob*. Rachel, the beloved, is buried elsewhere. This detail is often overlooked, but it speaks volumes. In death, Leah rests where covenant rests. In legacy, Leah is honored where promise is remembered.

Why Leah Matters

The God Who Sees the Overlooked

Leah matters because she represents the women who do everything right and still feel passed over. She speaks to those who love faithfully without being celebrated. She embodies the truth that productivity is not the same as fulfillment—and yet God can redeem even the emptiest places.

Leah teaches that praise can become a turning point. That identity does not have to be negotiated through rejection. That fruitfulness does not require applause. She shows us that God often builds His greatest work in the lives no one is applauding.

Leah's story corrects a dangerous lie—that being loved by people is proof of being favored by God. Sometimes the opposite is true. Sometimes God is closest to the ones who have no choice but to rely on Him.

Leah lived unseen by her husband, overshadowed by her sister, and underestimated by circumstance. Yet she became the matriarch of kings, priests, and promise.

She was not the favorite.
She was foundational.

And her life still speaks to women who are learning—slowly, bravely—that being overlooked by people does not mean being overlooked by God.

A Message from Leah

I speak to you as a woman who learned how to stay when leaving would have been easier. I speak as one who lived inside a marriage that did not begin with affection and did not always offer tenderness. I know what it is to be chosen by covenant and overlooked by emotion. I know the ache of sharing a life with someone whose heart seems to rest elsewhere.

Respect the marriage covenant. Do not treat it as something fragile that can be abandoned whenever feelings shift. Covenant is not sustained by emotion alone—it is carried by faithfulness, endurance, and obedience to God. I stayed not because every day felt good, but because staying mattered. I understood that marriage is not only about how love feels, but about what love builds.

Do not walk away simply because your heart is hurting. Pain does not mean God has left you. Silence does not mean your obedience is unseen. There were nights I lay beside a man who did not long for me, mornings I rose knowing my devotion was not returned in equal measure. Yet I remained. And in remaining, God met me.

I will tell you this gently, because it is true: favor does not always come in the form you expect. I wanted Jacob's love. God gave me fruitfulness. I wanted affection. God gave me legacy. I wanted to be chosen above another woman. God chose my womb to carry nations.

Do not despise what God is producing in you simply because it does not look like what you asked for. I learned to turn my longing into prayer and my disappointment into praise. When I named my son Judah, I stopped asking for my husband to see me and began praising God for seeing me Himself. That was the moment my spirit rose, even if my circumstances did not immediately change.

Honor covenant even when it stretches you. Honor it with your words, your posture, your patience. Do not poison your household with bitterness or contempt. What you nurture will grow. I nurtured faithfulness, and God nurtured destiny through me.

You may feel overshadowed. You may feel second. You may feel unseen. But hear me clearly: God builds His greatest works in quiet, faithful places. He placed kings and priests in my lineage not because I was favored by man, but because I was faithful before Him.

I am Leah.

I was not the beloved—but I was the builder.

I was not the favorite—but I was fruitful.

Stay.

Trust.

Praise.

God will bring favor in His time, and it will be deeper, stronger, and more enduring than the love you thought you needed to survive.

Lessons I will Take from Leah

_____

_____

_____

_____

_____

_____

_____

_____

_____

Chapter 5: Rachel

The Beloved Woman Whose Tears Still Echo

Rachel enters Scripture in a moment of tenderness and electricity—a meeting at a well where love arrives suddenly, unmistakably, and with consequence. Jacob sees her and moves the stone himself, an act of strength driven not by duty but by desire. For Rachel, this moment marks the beginning of a life both deeply loved and deeply wounded, cherished and challenged, remembered for beauty yet defined by longing.

She is the woman Jacob loves first and longest, the wife for whom he works fourteen years, the beloved whose name lingers in his heart even as time takes its toll.

Rachel's beauty is noted plainly in Scripture, but it is not vanity that shapes her story. It is expectation. Rachel grows up knowing she is desirable, chosen, wanted. She likely assumes motherhood will come as naturally as affection. Instead, her life becomes a slow unraveling of assumptions—proof that being loved does not protect a woman from sorrow, and being favored does not guarantee fulfillment.

Rachel and Jacob

Love That Endures Delay

Jacob's love for Rachel is not symbolic; it is personal and persistent. He works seven years for her, and Scripture says the time seems but a few days because of his love. When Laban deceives him and gives Leah instead, Jacob's heartbreak is sharp. Rachel becomes the wife he must wait for, the promise delayed, the woman whose absence defines his disappointment.

When Rachel finally becomes his wife, she carries Jacob's affection fully—but affection alone cannot heal the ache she carries inside. Leah's womb opens again and again, while Rachel's remains silent. And this is where Rachel's story becomes deeply human and painfully relatable. She is loved, yet barren. Desired, yet empty. Chosen, yet unfulfilled.

Rachel watches her sister bear sons while she bears nothing but waiting. The rivalry between them intensifies, fueled by comparison and grief. Rachel's envy is not cruelty—it is desperation. In a world where a woman's worth is often measured by her children, Rachel feels herself fading. Her cry to Jacob—*"Give me children, or I die"*—is not exaggeration. It is a woman naming the depth of her despair.

Jacob's response is sharp, almost impatient. Love does not always translate into understanding. Rachel learns that even a beloved wife can feel alone in her pain. She turns to strategy, offering her servant Bilhah to Jacob, hoping to claim children through another body. It is a decision born of anguish rather than faith, and it brings her sons—but not peace. Motherhood by proxy does not quiet the ache of barrenness; it only complicates it.

The Weight of Comparison

Sisters at War With Longing

Rachel's relationship with Leah is one of the most emotionally layered in Scripture. They are sisters bound by blood and divided by circumstance. Leah has children but no affection. Rachel has affection but no children. Each sister lives with what the other desires most. Their rivalry is not petty; it is a battle for identity, security, and worth.

Rachel's envy is visible. She bargains for mandrakes, hoping they might unlock fertility. She competes for nights with Jacob.

She watches Leah's belly grow while her own remains still. Yet even in rivalry, there is shared suffering. Both women are shaped by Laban's manipulation. Both are wives navigating a household built on tension and comparison. Rachel's pain simply speaks louder because her longing remains unmet longer.

God Remembers Rachel

When Silence Breaks

Scripture tells us plainly: *God remembered Rachel.* That sentence carries enormous weight. It does not say God finally noticed her. It says He remembered—implying she had always been seen, even in silence. Her womb opens not because of desperation, bargaining, or strategy, but because God acts.

Rachel conceives and bears Joseph, naming him with hope rather than bitterness. His name reflects her faith that God will add again. Motherhood transforms her posture. The woman who once cried in despair now names her son with expectation. Joseph becomes the child of her joy, the son who carries her affection and later Jacob's deepest pride.

Later, Rachel conceives again. This pregnancy carries both promise and peril. As Jacob's household journeys, Rachel goes into hard labor on the road. There is no tent prepared, no comfort arranged. Her body, long denied fruitfulness, now carries life at great cost.

She names her son Ben-Oni—*son of my sorrow*—as life leaves her body. Jacob renames the child Benjamin—*son of my right hand*—refusing to let death define the legacy of her final breath. Rachel dies bringing life into the world, her story closing as painfully as it opened beautifully.

Rachel's Death and Jacob's Grief

Love That Does Not Let Go

Rachel's death wounds Jacob deeply. He buries her on the way to Ephrath and sets a pillar over her grave. She is not buried in the family tomb like Leah. She rests along the road—yet even there, her memory is preserved. Rachel becomes a symbol of sorrow and compassion in Israel's collective memory. Scripture later speaks of Rachel weeping for her children, her voice echoing through generations.

What Rachel meant to Jacob cannot be overstated. She is the wife he never stopped loving, the one whose loss lingered. Even years later, as Jacob blesses his sons, Rachel's children— Joseph and Benjamin—hold a unique place in his heart. Love does not erase grief; it sanctifies it. Rachel remains beloved even in absence.

Why Rachel Matters

The Ache That Shapes Legacy

Rachel matters because she speaks to women whose lives look full but feel empty. She represents those who are loved yet unfulfilled, admired yet aching, chosen yet waiting. Her story reminds us that longing is not a lack of faith, and envy is often a cry for dignity rather than malice.

She teaches us that silence is not abandonment. That God remembers even when time stretches painfully long. That motherhood does not arrive on our schedule, and fulfillment does not always come without cost.

Rachel's life is a reminder that being beloved does not shield us from sorrow—but it does mean our tears are remembered. Her legacy lives not only through her sons, but through the honesty of her longing. She is proof that beauty does not cancel pain, love does not prevent loss, and faith can coexist with desperation.

Rachel was beloved.
Rachel was barren.
Rachel was remembered.

And through her, Scripture tells the truth women still live today: sometimes the deepest love is paired with the deepest ache—but God is present in both, shaping a legacy that stretches far beyond one lifetime.

A Message from Rachel

I speak to you as a woman who was deeply loved and still deeply broken. Do not believe the lie that love alone protects you from longing. I was cherished, chosen, waited for—and still I waited. Still I wept. Still I learned that God does not rush simply because our hearts are aching.

Have patience. Not the quiet patience that pretends not to feel, but the living patience that breathes through tears and keeps standing anyway. Some things with God are not instant—not because He is slow, but because what He is shaping in you cannot be rushed without breaking you. I wanted children immediately. I wanted my joy to arrive when love did. It did not. And that delay taught me that timing is not punishment; it is preparation.

Guard your integrity while you wait. I did not always do this well. I compared myself to my sister. I let envy speak louder than gratitude. I reached for solutions that brought movement but not peace. Learn from me—do not let desperation rewrite your values. What you obtain outside of God's timing may give you relief for a moment, but it will not heal the ache you are trying to silence.

Do not measure your worth by what is slow to come. I learned too late how easily a woman can disappear inside comparison. I had love, beauty, position—and still I felt invisible because I lacked one thing. Do not let one unanswered prayer cancel the goodness God has already placed in your life. Gratitude is a discipline, not a feeling.

And hear this with tenderness: silence does not mean God has forgotten you. Scripture says God remembered me. That means He saw me the whole time—even when my womb was closed, even when my prayers felt unanswered, even when my faith faltered. God remembers women who are waiting. He remembers tears shed in private. He remembers the ache you cannot explain without breaking down.

When fulfillment came, it came with weight. Joy does not always arrive gently. Sometimes it costs us more than we expected. Life is holy even when it is painful. If my story teaches you anything, let it be this: God is present in the waiting *and* in the sorrow. Love does not end because life is hard. Meaning does not disappear because the road is long.

Be patient. Be faithful. Be whole even while you wait.
Do not abandon yourself in the delay.
Do not abandon God because He works slowly.

I am Rachel.
I was loved.
I waited.
I was remembered.

And so will you be.

Lessons I will Take from Rachel

_____

_____

_____

_____

_____

_____

_____

_____

_____

Chapter 6: Jochebed

The Woman Who Trusted God When
Fear Ruled the World

Jochebed's life unfolds in the shadow of empire. She is born into a time when power wears cruelty like a crown and oppression is written into law. Egypt is strong. Israel is enslaved. Hebrew bodies are counted, controlled, and crushed beneath fear. Pharaoh's command is ruthless: every

Hebrew son must die. This is the world Jochebed inhabits—a world where motherhood is dangerous and hope feels reckless.

And yet, Jochebed becomes a mother anyway.

She does not enter Scripture as a public leader or a woman with status. She enters as a wife and a mother—ordinary roles made extraordinary by the weight of her obedience. She is married to Amram, a man of the tribe of Levi, and together they build a family in a land determined to erase them. They already have children—Miriam and Aaron—when Jochebed becomes pregnant again. This child will be born under a death sentence.

Scripture tells us that when Jochebed sees her son, she sees that he is "a goodly child." But this goodness is more than physical beauty. It is spiritual recognition. Jochebed perceives destiny before it has a name. Where Pharaoh sees a threat, Jochebed sees promise. Where the law demands surrender, her spirit responds with faith.

Faith in Hiding

A Mother's Quiet Resistance

For three months, Jochebed hides her son. This is not a passive act. It is resistance wrapped in tenderness. Every cry must be quieted. Every movement must be measured. Every day carries the risk of discovery and death. Jochebed lives with fear breathing down her neck, yet she refuses to let fear make her faith small.

But there comes a moment when hiding is no longer enough. The baby grows. His voice strengthens. The walls cannot protect him forever. Jochebed reaches a crossroads that every faithful parent eventually faces: she must release what she loves into God's hands or watch it be destroyed by forces she cannot control.

Her decision is as daring as it is devastating.

She builds a basket of bulrushes, waterproofed with slime and pitch—not hastily, but carefully. Faith, in Jochebed's hands, is practical. She places her son inside and sets him among the reeds of the Nile. This is not abandonment. It is offering. The same river meant to swallow Hebrew sons becomes the vehicle of deliverance because Jochebed trusts God enough to believe He can meet her child where she cannot go.

She sends Miriam to watch from a distance—not out of fear alone, but out of wisdom. Jochebed does not surrender responsibility when she surrenders control. She stays engaged. She stays alert. She stays hopeful.

God's Irony and a Mother's Reward

Deliverance from the House of the Enemy

Pharaoh's daughter finds the child. The irony is holy. The very household that ordered Hebrew sons to die becomes the place where Israel's deliverer is preserved. When the princess hears the baby cry, compassion interrupts cruelty. Jochebed's faith meets divine timing.

Through Miriam's bold intervention, Jochebed is called to nurse her own child—paid by the empire that sought his death. She is given back what she released. This moment is more than emotional restoration; it is prophetic justice. God honors Jochebed's obedience by allowing her to shape the early years of the one who will shape history.

During that sacred time, Jochebed pours identity into Moses before Egypt can rename him. She teaches him who he is, where he comes from, and whose he belongs to. She does not have long, but she has enough. Enough to root him in truth. Enough to anchor him in covenant. Enough to ensure that when Moses grows up in Pharaoh's palace, he will still hear the echo of his mother's faith.

A Legacy Beyond One Child

The Power of Faithful Obedience

Jochebed's impact does not end with Moses. Her household becomes the nucleus of Israel's deliverance. Aaron will speak. Miriam will prophesy. Moses will lead. But behind all three stands a mother who trusted God when obedience carried unbearable cost.

Jochebed does not lead Israel out of Egypt with a staff—but she makes the staff-holder possible. She does not confront Pharaoh with plagues—but she confronts fear with faith. Her contribution is not loud, but it is foundational. Without her courage, there is no Exodus.

She shows us that deliverance often begins in private decisions no one applauds. That faith does not always look like triumph—it sometimes looks like release. That a mother's obedience can outlive her lifetime and alter the destiny of nations.

Why Jochebed Matters

Faith That Refuses to Bow to Fear

Jochebed matters because she represents believers who remain faithful under pressure. She speaks to women who are raising children in hostile systems, to parents who must trust God with outcomes they cannot control, to those who love deeply in dangerous times.

She teaches us that trust is not passive—it is active courage. That faith is not denial of danger—it is obedience in spite of it. That God specializes in turning instruments of death into channels of life.

Jochebed never sees the Red Sea part. She never hears the law thunder from Sinai. She never watches Egypt fall beneath judgment. Yet her obedience makes all of it possible. Her life reminds us that you do not have to witness the fulfillment of God's promise to be essential to it.

Jochebed is a woman of hidden faith, quiet bravery, and immeasurable impact. She trusted God with her child when the world demanded his death—and God entrusted her child with the liberation of an entire people.

She stands as a witness across generations:
that oppression does not cancel purpose,
that fear does not negate faith,
and that obedience—when offered fully—can change the course of history.

A Message from Jochebed

I speak to you as a woman who learned how to breathe under pressure. I learned how to love while laws were written against my children. I learned how to trust God when power said my people did not deserve to live. If you are weary from carrying dignity through systems designed to strip it away, then hear me—I know this road.

Endure. Not because oppression is acceptable, but because your endurance is an act of resistance. I lived beneath decrees that targeted my sons, under a regime that feared our future and tried to erase it. Yet fear did not become my god. Courage did not leave me. I refused to let cruelty dictate my obedience to the Most High.

You will face racism. You will face structures that profit from your silence and benefit from your exhaustion. Do not internalize their hatred. Their fear of you is not evidence of your inferiority—it is proof of your potential. Pharaoh feared what would rise from our wombs. Oppression always fears what it cannot control.

Maintain your courage. Courage is not loud defiance every day; sometimes it is quiet consistency. Sometimes it is nurturing life in a hostile world. Sometimes it is teaching truth before lies can take root. Sometimes it is releasing what you love into God's hands when the world gives you no safe place to hold it.

I did not abandon my son—I entrusted him. There is a difference. I placed him where I could not follow because I believed God could go where I could not. Faith will sometimes require you to let go without knowing how the story ends. Do not confuse that release with weakness. It is one of the strongest acts a woman can perform.

Teach your children who they are before the world teaches them who they are not. I had little time, but I used it well. Identity can survive palaces if it is rooted early. Truth can live in exile if it is planted deep. What you pour into the next generation matters more than the systems they are born into.

Do not believe that your obedience is small because it is unseen. I did not part seas. I did not call down plagues. I obeyed in a kitchen, in a hidden room, beside a river. And yet my obedience became the doorway through which deliverance entered history. God builds liberation through faithful women long before it appears on a public stage.

If you are tired, rest—but do not surrender your spirit. If you are angry, bring it to God—but do not let it consume your purpose. If you are afraid, walk anyway. Fear does not disqualify you. Silence does not mean God is absent. Oppression does not cancel calling.

I am Jochebed.
I mothered hope under tyranny.
I trusted God when the world demanded despair.

Endure.
Be brave.
Keep believing.

Your faith—quiet, steady, unrelenting—may be the very thing that delivers generations you will never live to see.

Lessons I will Take from Jochebed

_____

_____

_____

_____

_____

_____

_____

_____

_____

Chapter 7: Miriam

The Woman Who Watched, Sang,
Spoke and Learned

Miriam's story begins before she ever lifts a song. It begins with watching. With stillness. With courage disguised as a child's quiet obedience. Long before Israel would know her as prophetess, long before her voice would lead a nation in praise, Miriam learns how to stand guard over destiny without drawing attention to herself.

She is a daughter of slaves in a land that profits from their suffering. Egypt's cruelty presses down on her people, and Pharaoh's decree hangs like a blade over every Hebrew household: sons must die. In this world, Miriam grows up quickly. Fear matures children faster than time ever could. And when her mother, Jochebed, prepares a basket for the Nile, Miriam becomes part of an act of faith that will ripple through history.

The Watchful Sister

Faith Learned in Silence

Miriam helps her mother place her baby brother into the basket. Scripture does not describe her hands trembling, but we can feel the weight of the moment. She knows the river is dangerous. She knows soldiers patrol. She knows what happens to boys like her brother. Yet she agrees to watch. Not to interfere—just to be present. Presence, in moments like this, is its own form of bravery.

She stands at a distance, eyes fixed on the reeds, heart beating with prayer she has not yet learned to name. When Pharaoh's daughter approaches and discovers the crying child, Miriam does not freeze. She steps forward with wisdom beyond her years, offering a solution that brings her own mother back into the story. In one moment of courage and clarity, Miriam becomes a bridge between oppression and mercy.

This is Miriam's first recorded act: she watches over deliverance before deliverance has a name.

Growing Into Calling

From Observer to Prophetess

Miriam does not fade into the background after Moses is saved. She grows into her calling alongside her brothers— Moses and Aaron—each carrying a distinct role in God's unfolding plan. Where Moses speaks to Pharaoh and Aaron speaks to the people, Miriam speaks to the soul of the nation.

Scripture names her plainly: *Miriam the prophetess.* This title is not honorary. It is earned. Miriam hears God. She understands His movement among the people. She recognizes the moment when history turns.

After the Red Sea closes over Egypt's power and Israel stands on the far shore—free for the first time—Miriam takes her timbrel in hand. She does not wait for instruction. She does not defer celebration to the men. She leads. She calls the women forward and lifts a song of victory that echoes Moses' words but carries its own authority. Her praise is embodied, communal, unrestrained. It is joy after terror, release after generations of bondage.

Miriam understands something vital: freedom must be celebrated or it will be forgotten. Her song seals deliverance into memory.

Leadership, Visibility, and Tension

When Familiarity Breeds Doubt

Miriam's proximity to Moses brings both strength and strain. She knows him not only as prophet, but as brother. She remembers the basket. The river. The boy who once needed watching. And familiarity can be both grounding and dangerous.

When Moses marries a Cushite woman, Miriam—along with Aaron—questions him. The issue is layered: personal concern, cultural discomfort, and spiritual jealousy intertwine. Miriam asks a dangerous question: *Has the Lord spoken only through Moses? Has He not spoken through us also?*

It is a question born of closeness and comparison. Of siblings who have walked together through trauma and triumph and now struggle to remain aligned as roles diverge. Miriam's mistake is not ambition; it is forgetting that calling does not require competition.

God responds swiftly and publicly. Miriam is struck with leprosy, her skin reflecting the internal fracture that had taken root. The punishment is severe—but so is the love. Moses intercedes for her immediately. The people stop moving until she is restored. Israel does not journey without Miriam.

This moment matters deeply. It shows that leadership includes accountability. That prophetic voices are not exempt from correction. And that even when Miriam falters, she remains essential.

Restoration and Honor

A Community That Waits

Miriam's restoration is quiet but powerful. After seven days outside the camp, she is brought back. There is no recorded speech, no public apology, no dramatic reinstatement. Yet the people wait for her. That waiting is honor. It acknowledges her role, her value, her place.

She returns not diminished, but tempered. Miriam continues to walk with the nation, carrying both wisdom and humility. She knows now that leadership must be guarded by reverence, and that intimacy with God does not cancel the need for obedience.

Miriam's Legacy

The Woman Who Taught Israel to Sing

Miriam dies in the wilderness, in Kadesh. Scripture records her death simply, without flourish. But the absence she leaves behind is immediately felt. The people soon find themselves without water—a symbolic echo of the woman who once stood watch over life at the river's edge. Miriam's presence had been sustaining in ways few recognized until she was gone.

She is remembered not only as Moses' sister, but as a leader in her own right. As a prophetess. As a worshiper. As a woman whose voice shaped the emotional and spiritual life of Israel.

Miriam teaches us that deliverance requires witnesses, worship, and women willing to stand at the edges of danger with faith in their eyes. She shows us that leadership is not linear—that even the called can stumble, and even correction can lead to deeper purpose.

She watched when watching mattered. She sang when singing sealed freedom. She spoke when silence would have betrayed calling. And she learned when humility was required.

Miriam's life reminds us that God uses women not only to birth deliverers, but to guard them, guide them, and give voice to the joy of liberation. She stands in Scripture as proof that faith can begin in childhood, mature through leadership, be refined through correction, and still finish strong—leaving a song behind that generations will remember.

A Message from Miriam

Sisters—come closer. Let me talk to you, standing on cracked ground with dust on my feet and truth in my mouth.

I know what it is to grow up under pressure. I know what it feels like to be watched, counted, controlled. I was born into a system that decided my people were dangerous just for existing. They called us a problem. They made laws about our bodies, our sons, our future. So if you're tired of racism, tired of oppression, tired of feeling like the world stays heavy no matter how hard you work—believe me, I know that weight.

Endure. Not quietly. Not broken. Endure with your back straight and your eyes open. Endure knowing that survival itself is holy. I stood on the riverbank when death was legal and hope was illegal. I watched my baby brother float between fear and destiny. And I didn't run. Courage doesn't always roar—sometimes it stands still and refuses to look away.

Keep your courage. Don't let bitterness steal your voice. Don't let exhaustion convince you that silence is safer. I learned early that God moves through women who stay alert. Pay attention. Watch what God is doing in your family, in your neighborhood, in your children. Sometimes deliverance comes wrapped in danger, and you have to recognize it before anyone else does.

And when God brings you through—*sing*. I mean that. Celebrate out loud. Dance when chains break. Praise when systems fall. I grabbed my tambourine on the far side of the Red Sea because freedom needs a soundtrack. If you don't praise it, you might forget it. Joy is resistance. Celebration is protest. Don't let anybody tell you worship has to be quiet or polite.

But let me be real with you too. Even leaders mess up. Even strong women stumble. I questioned my brother when I shouldn't have. Familiarity made me forget reverence. Pride tried to slip in where purpose lived. And God corrected me— not to destroy me, but to refine me. So if you've ever let jealousy, comparison, or frustration get the better of you— don't quit. Get corrected. Get humble. Get back up.

And hear this: when I fell, the people *waited* for me. The whole camp stopped moving until I was restored. That's how you know you matter—even when you mess up. Don't let shame tell you you're disposable. God doesn't discard women who helped carry the vision just because they had a weak moment.

Stay connected to your sisters. Sing together. Watch out for each other's children. Speak up when something ain't right. Liberation was never meant to be solo. We crossed that sea together.

I'm Miriam.
I watched when watching was dangerous.
I sang when singing sealed freedom.
I endured correction and kept walking anyway.

So you—
Endure.
Stay loud.
Stay faithful.
Stay courageous.

And when God brings you through something the world said you wouldn't survive—make sure somebody hears your song.

Lessons I will Take from Miriam

_____

_____

_____

_____

_____

_____

_____

_____

_____

Chapter 8: Naomi

The Woman Who Lost Everything—and Still Led Another Home

Naomi's life reads like a slow unraveling, the kind that happens quietly, one loss at a time, until a woman looks up and barely recognizes herself. She is not introduced as a heroine or a prophetess, but as a wife and a mother—secure, rooted, ordinary in the best sense of the word. She begins her story in Bethlehem, the "house of bread," surrounded by family, familiarity, and faith. And then famine comes, and with it the first hard decision.

Naomi leaves the land of promise not because she stops believing in God, but because survival demands movement. Alongside her husband, Elimelech, she journeys to Moab, a foreign land heavy with tension and difference. This is not rebellion—it is desperation. Naomi is a woman doing what countless women have done across generations: choosing displacement over starvation, uncertainty over death.

In Moab, Naomi becomes a stranger. She watches her sons grow into men and marry Moabite women—Ruth and Orpah—unions that blend cultures and test assumptions. For a moment, life stabilizes. And then everything collapses.

First Elimelech dies.

Naomi becomes a widow in a foreign land—a vulnerable position in any era, but especially in one where male protection often meant survival. Still, she has her sons. Still, she has hope. And then, one by one, her sons die too. Mahlon. Chilion. Gone. The names remain, but the voices disappear.

Naomi is left with her grief and her daughters-in-law—three widows bound together by loss and uncertainty. Scripture does not rush past this pain. Ten years pass in Moab, and Naomi's sorrow settles deep. This is not a quick tragedy; it is prolonged emptiness. She has no husband, no sons, no future lineage, and no homeland that feels close enough to touch.

"Call Me Mara"

When Faith Tells the Truth About Pain

When Naomi hears that the Lord has visited His people again with bread, she decides to return home. Not because she is healed—but because staying in Moab no longer makes sense. Naomi understands something vital: grief may follow you anywhere, but healing often begins when you turn back toward where you belong.

She urges her daughters-in-law to stay behind, to rebuild their lives where they still have cultural footing. Orpah weeps and returns. Ruth refuses. Ruth clings.

Naomi does not romanticize her faith. She does not offer Ruth easy optimism or sugar-coated hope. She speaks honestly: her life feels empty. She believes God's hand has gone out against her. When she arrives in Bethlehem, the women recognize her and gasp—but Naomi interrupts their joy.

"Do not call me Naomi," she says. "Call me Mara. Bitter."

This moment matters. Naomi's faith is not performative. She does not pretend her pain is smaller than it is. She does not deny loss to appear spiritual. She names her grief without abandoning God. Lament, in Naomi's life, becomes an act of faith—not rebellion.

Naomi and Ruth

Love That Refuses to Leave

Naomi's relationship with Ruth is one of the most tender and powerful bonds in Scripture. Ruth chooses Naomi not out of obligation, but out of love and conviction. "Where you go, I will go. Your people will be my people. Your God, my God."

Naomi does not ask for this loyalty—but she receives it. And slowly, quietly, Naomi begins to lead again—not through authority, but through wisdom earned by suffering. She guides Ruth into the fields to glean. She recognizes Boaz as a kinsman-redeemer before Ruth understands the significance. She instructs Ruth with care, dignity, and strategy—not manipulation.

This is Naomi's redemption arc: she moves from despair to discernment. From bitterness to hope. From passive grief to active participation in God's restoration. Naomi never remarries. She never bears another child. Yet her influence shapes the future in ways she could never have imagined.

When Ruth marries Boaz and bears a son, the women of Bethlehem gather again—but this time, their words are different. They bless Naomi. They place the child in her arms. They say that Ruth, who loves her, is better to her than seven sons.

Naomi becomes a nurturer once more—not of what she lost, but of what God restored in a new form.

Restoration Without Erasure

Joy That Does Not Cancel Grief

Naomi's story does not end with denial of pain. Her losses are not erased. Elimelech does not return. Her sons remain buried in Moab. But redemption enters her life without asking her to forget what she endured. That is the beauty of Naomi's restoration: it is honest.

She becomes grandmother to Obed—the grandfather of David, ancestor of kings, and part of the lineage that will lead to the Messiah. Naomi, once convinced her life was over, becomes a link in the chain of redemption history.

Her hands that once trembled with emptiness now hold promise.

Why Naomi Matters

Faith That Survives the Worst

Naomi matters because she speaks to women who have buried dreams, relationships, seasons, and identities. She represents those who feel like life has taken more than it gave back. She reminds us that bitterness does not disqualify faith—and honesty does not offend God.

She teaches that leadership can look like guidance instead of command. That wisdom can be born from grief. That restoration may come through people you never expected— sometimes through the very ones you once tried to send away.

Naomi's faith does not sparkle. It endures. It limps home. It tells the truth. And in doing so, it makes room for redemption.

She lost everything.
She told the truth about it.
And God rebuilt her legacy anyway.

Naomi's life assures us that even when you return empty, God is still writing the ending.

A Message from Naomi

Daughter, come sit with me for a moment. Let me speak to you from the far side of loss, from the place where tears have already fallen and faith has had to learn how to walk with a limp.

I know what it is to bury the people you thought would bury you. I know what it is to wake up one day and realize the life you planned no longer exists. Husband gone. Sons gone. Future emptied out so suddenly it steals the air from your lungs. If you are carrying grief that has reshaped you, if you are learning how to live after death has visited your house—I understand you.

Endure. Not because the pain is small, but because God is still present inside it. Endurance does not mean pretending you are strong. It means choosing not to disappear. I returned home with nothing but my name and my sorrow, and even then I wondered if God had turned His face away. I told the truth about my bitterness. I did not hide it. And still—God stayed.

Hear this clearly: God will never leave you. Not in the land of plenty. Not in famine. Not in foreign places. Not in graveside silence. I felt empty, but I was not abandoned. I felt broken, but I was not forgotten. God walks with women who are grieving just as surely as He walks with women who are rejoicing.

Do not rush yourself to heal. Do not let anyone shame your sorrow or hurry your process. Loss changes you, and that is not a failure—it is a passage. I learned that faith does not always sing; sometimes it limps. Sometimes it whispers. Sometimes it simply takes one more step toward home.

Pay attention to who stays with you. I tried to send Ruth away because I believed I had nothing left to give. I was wrong. God often sends loyalty when we think we are too empty to receive it. Do not despise companionship in your grief. Let love walk beside you, even when you cannot yet imagine joy again.

And remember this: restoration does not always look like replacement. God did not give me back what I lost—but He gave me new purpose. He placed life in my arms again, not through my own womb, but through legacy. The ending I thought I deserved was not the ending He was writing.

If your heart feels bitter, tell God. If your hands feel empty, bring them anyway. If your future feels uncertain, keep walking toward where you belong. Redemption often meets us on the road back, not at the place of our deepest pain.

I am Naomi.
I lost much.
I told the truth about it.
And God did not leave me there.

So endure, daughter.
Grieve honestly.
Walk forward slowly.

God is still with you—and the story is not over yet.

Lessons I will Take from Naomi

_____

_____

_____

_____

_____

_____

_____

_____

_____

Chapter 9: Ruth

*The Woman Who Chose Love—and
Stepped Into Destiny*

Ruth's story does not begin with promise. It begins with loss. With burial soil still fresh and a future suddenly narrowed by grief. She is a Moabite woman, raised outside the covenant, shaped by a people often viewed with suspicion and distance by Israel. She does not grow up expecting her name to be remembered. She does not imagine herself stitched into sacred lineage. Ruth enters Scripture as a widow—young, vulnerable, and expendable by the standards of the world she inhabits.

And yet, Ruth will become one of the most profound witnesses of faithfulness the Bible has ever preserved.

Her life teaches us that destiny is not inherited by blood alone, but by choice. By loyalty. By love that refuses to turn back when leaving would be easier.

Ruth and Naomi

Love That Refused to Let Go

Ruth's defining moment does not happen in a field or at a gate—it happens on a road. Naomi, broken by the deaths of her husband and sons, prepares to return to Bethlehem. She urges her daughters-in-law to stay behind, to rebuild their lives where familiarity still exists. Naomi believes she has nothing left to offer. No future. No protection. No joy.

Orpah leaves in tears. Ruth stays.

Ruth's words are not dramatic—they are deliberate. *Where you go, I will go. Where you lodge, I will lodge. Your people shall be my people, and your God my God.* This is not youthful impulse. It is covenant language spoken without ceremony. Ruth binds herself not only to Naomi, but to Naomi's God, Naomi's grief, Naomi's uncertain future.

In that moment, Ruth becomes more than a daughter-in-law. She becomes a companion in sorrow. A carrier of hope Naomi cannot yet imagine for herself. Ruth chooses love when love offers no guarantees.

A Faith That Works

Providence in Ordinary Obedience

When Ruth arrives in Bethlehem, she does not wait to be rescued. She goes to glean in the fields—doing the humblest work available to survive. This is where Ruth's faith becomes visible. She trusts God not through grand declarations, but through steady action. She moves. She works. She shows up.

Providence meets her steps quietly.

She happens to glean in the field of Boaz, a man of standing and kindness, a relative of Naomi's late husband. Scripture never frames this as coincidence—it is divine orchestration unfolding through ordinary obedience. Ruth's humility draws favor. Her reputation for loyalty precedes her. Boaz has heard how she left everything to care for Naomi, how she chose covenant over convenience.

Ruth does not manipulate attention. She does not demand reward. She receives kindness with gratitude and dignity. Her character becomes her covering.

Love That Transforms

From Stranger to Redeemed

Naomi, slowly awakening from despair, recognizes opportunity. She guides Ruth—not recklessly, but wisely—toward redemption through Boaz as kinsman-redeemer. Ruth follows instruction with courage and integrity. Her actions at the threshing floor are bold, but not immoral. They are symbolic, respectful, and rooted in covenant law.

Boaz responds not with exploitation, but with honor. He protects Ruth's reputation and commits to redeem her properly. Love, in this story, does not rush. It does not violate order. It fulfills it.

Ruth becomes a wife not because she is rescued, but because she is redeemed. Her marriage to Boaz restores her social standing, her security, and her future. But the transformation does not stop with her.

Inclusion in the Promise

Grace Beyond Bloodlines

Ruth bears a son—Obed. The women of Bethlehem rejoice, not only for Ruth, but for Naomi. Life returns to hands once empty. Joy settles where bitterness once lived. Ruth, the foreigner, becomes the means through which Naomi's legacy is restored.

Obed becomes the father of Jesse, the father of David. And through David's line will come the Messiah—Jesus Christ. Ruth, the Moabite widow, becomes woven into the very heart of redemption history.

Her inclusion is revolutionary. Ruth's life declares that God's covenant is not confined to ethnicity, background, or past identity. Faithfulness opens doors bloodlines never could. Love becomes the language God honors.

Why Ruth Matters

The Power of Choosing Love

Ruth matters because she shows us that faith can be quiet and still be fierce. That loyalty can be a form of worship. That love—when chosen selflessly—can reshape history.

She never preaches. Never commands. Never leads armies. Yet her obedience alters lineage. Her devotion brings restoration. Her love becomes a bridge between nations, between sorrow and joy, between exclusion and inclusion.

Ruth teaches us that God watches how we treat the vulnerable, how we care for the grieving, how we respond when no one is promising us anything in return. She reminds us that redemption often begins with a decision to stay.

She was not born into the promise.
She chose it.

And because she chose love, she became part of a story far greater than herself—one that would bless generations she would never live to see.

Ruth's life still speaks:
that faithfulness is powerful,
that providence walks beside obedience,
and that love—when rooted in God—has the power to transform not only individual lives, but the very course of history.

A Message from Ruth

I speak to you as a woman who chose to stay when leaving would have been easier. I did not follow Naomi because life promised me reward. I followed her because love asked me to. Sometimes faith does not shout—it walks beside someone who is grieving and refuses to let them walk alone.

Be faithful to the people God has placed in your life. Loyalty is not weakness. It is strength exercised quietly. I bound myself to Naomi when she believed she had nothing left to give. I learned that love is not proven in abundance, but in scarcity. If you can remain when joy has disappeared, you carry a kind of faith that heaven recognizes.

Do not despise humble work. I gleaned in fields not knowing who watched or why it mattered. I worked because survival required it, and dignity demanded it. Providence met me there. God often arranges destiny in places that look ordinary and feel unseen. Show up anyway. Faithfulness in small things opens doors you did not know existed.

When love found me again, it came with honor. Boaz did not rush me or misuse my vulnerability. He covered me with respect and followed God's order. Learn this: real love protects your name. It does not require you to abandon your integrity. It waits, redeems, and restores. If love asks you to lose yourself, it is not from God.

Trust God's timing. I was a widow before I was a wife again. A foreigner before I became family. Do not rush what God is redeeming. Let love grow in safety, patience, and truth. The right relationships will recognize your worth without you having to announce it.

And remember—you do not have to be born into promise to belong to it. I was an outsider, yet God made room for me. Faithfulness brought me into a lineage I never imagined. Love became my language, and God answered it with legacy.

I am Ruth.
I stayed when leaving made sense.
I worked when no one noticed.
I loved with integrity.

Be faithful.
Walk humbly.
Trust God's unfolding.

You never know how far obedience, wrapped in love, will carry you.

Lessons I will Take from Ruth

_____

_____

_____

_____

_____

_____

_____

_____

_____

Chapter 10: Abigail

The Woman Who Intercepted Wrath and Altered a Kingdom

Abigail enters Scripture already complete. She is not introduced as a girl becoming wise, but as a woman who already is. The Bible says she is intelligent and beautiful—yet it is her discernment, not her appearance, that shapes history. She is married to Nabal, a man whose name means "fool," and whose character lives up to it. Where Abigail is thoughtful, Nabal is reckless. Where she is generous, he is harsh. Where she understands timing and consequence, he stumbles through life blind to both.

Abigail lives in a household marked by abundance without wisdom. Nabal is wealthy, prosperous, and powerful—but spiritually small. He benefits from protection he neither acknowledges nor appreciates. David and his men have guarded Nabal's shepherds in the wilderness, providing safety without demand. When David sends messengers requesting provision during a feast—a culturally reasonable request— Nabal responds with insult and contempt. He dismisses David as a nobody, a runaway servant, unworthy of honor.

It is not just a rude response. It is a dangerous one.

Discernment in Crisis

Wisdom That Moves Faster Than Pride

When Abigail hears what her husband has done, she does not panic. She does not argue with Nabal. She does not waste time trying to reform a man unwilling to listen. Abigail understands something critical: discernment requires action, not debate.

She moves quickly. She gathers bread, wine, meat, grain, raisins, and figs—abundance meant for celebration now repurposed for peacemaking. She goes out to meet David without her husband's knowledge, not out of deceit, but out of responsibility. Abigail knows the cost of delay. She knows bloodshed is moments away.

When she meets David, Abigail does not posture. She dismounts, bows, and speaks with humility that carries authority. Her words are careful, layered, and prophetic. She takes responsibility without claiming guilt. She acknowledges wrongdoing without excusing it. She appeals to David's destiny, reminding him that shedding innocent blood will stain the kingship God is forming in him.

Abigail sees David not as a fugitive, but as a future king. She speaks to who he will be, not just who he is in that heated moment. Her wisdom disarms anger. Her courage redirects violence. David listens.

And history turns.

The Power of a Woman Who Intervenes

Stopping Bloodshed Before It Begins

Abigail's intervention does more than save her household. It saves David from himself. It preserves his future from being marked by unnecessary blood. David blesses her discernment, acknowledging that God sent her to restrain him.

This is no small moment. Abigail stands between wrath and restraint, between impulse and inheritance. She does not wield a weapon—she wields wisdom. Her courage proves that discernment is not passive. It is decisive. It steps into danger when silence would be easier.

When Abigail returns home, she finds Nabal drunk and feasting, oblivious to how close he came to destruction. She waits until morning to tell him what happened. When he hears it, his heart fails within him. Ten days later, Nabal dies.

Scripture does not frame this as Abigail's revenge. It frames it as divine justice. God removes what Abigail could not change. Wisdom does not always fix foolishness—but it does survive it.

From Constrained to Crowned

The Rise of a Queen

After Nabal's death, David sends for Abigail. He recognizes what others already should have: her wisdom, her strength, her worth. Abigail accepts—not as a desperate widow seeking security, but as a woman stepping into alignment with God's unfolding plan.

She becomes David's wife, and eventually, royalty. But her elevation is not the point of her story—it is the consequence of her character. Abigail's discernment prepared her for queenship long before a crown ever touched her head.

As queen, Abigail brings to the palace what she carried in crisis: clarity, restraint, and wisdom. She understands leadership not as domination, but as responsibility. She understands that power without discernment destroys itself.

Why Abigail Matters

Wisdom That Saves Futures

Abigail matters because she shows what happens when a woman refuses to let someone else's foolishness dictate her destiny. She teaches that marriage to a difficult man does not erase a woman's agency. That wisdom can operate even under constraint. That discernment can protect generations yet unborn.

She reminds us that timing matters. That humility can stop violence. That speaking at the right moment can change the course of history. Abigail does not wait for permission to do what is right. She recognizes the moment—and she moves.

Her story speaks to women navigating environments shaped by ego, volatility, and unchecked pride. She shows that you do not need to match foolishness with foolishness. You can answer chaos with clarity. You can answer wrath with wisdom.

Abigail stands as proof that God honors discernment wherever it is found. That He elevates those who protect life, preserve integrity, and act courageously when stakes are high.

She was married to a fool,
but she was not foolish.

She lived in the shadow of recklessness,
but she carried the light of wisdom.

And because she acted when it mattered most,
she moved from survival to royalty—
not by ambition,
but by discernment that saved a king and shaped a kingdom.

A Message from Abigail

Let me speak plainly to you, sister—woman to woman, heart to heart.

I lived married to a man whose mouth moved faster than his wisdom. I knew what it was like to share a house with abundance and still feel the danger of foolishness hanging in the air. I did not choose my husband's character, but I chose my own. Hear me clearly: a woman's destiny is not erased because she is joined to a difficult man.

I did not divorce him. I did not expose him. I did not answer his foolishness with rebellion or shame. I *interceded*. I stepped into the gap when his pride invited destruction. Wisdom does not always shout; sometimes it moves quietly, urgently, and at great personal risk. I understood that one reckless moment could cost many lives—including his.

Do not confuse discernment with disrespect. I honored the covenant even while refusing to participate in destruction. I did not follow my husband into error, but I did not abandon him either. There is a difference between submission and surrendering your God-given wisdom. I kept my wit sharp, my spirit anchored, and my ear tuned to timing.

When danger came, I acted. I did not wait for permission to save lives. I bowed low, spoke truth, and appealed to destiny— not ego. I reminded David who he was becoming, not what anger was tempting him to be. Sometimes God positions a woman to stop bloodshed, to redirect a future, to intercept wrath before it stains legacy.

And listen to this part carefully: my obedience did not trap me—it *positioned* me. God removed what I could not change. He honored wisdom that protected life. I did not scheme my way into royalty. I walked in discernment, and destiny found me where I stood.

If you are married to a man who lacks wisdom, do not let bitterness turn you into someone you are not. Stay anchored. Stay discerning. Stay courageous. Your faithfulness is not wasted, even when it is unseen. God sees the woman who protects integrity when chaos is easier.

I am Abigail.
I lived with a fool, but I was not one.
I interceded instead of retaliating.
I trusted wisdom over impulse.

And God lifted me—not because I chased a crown,
but because I protected a future.

Walk wisely, sister.

Your discernment may be the very thing that saves lives—
and leads you into the destiny God has already prepared.

Lessons I will Take from Abigail

Chapter 11: Hannah

The Woman Who Turned Agony into Anointing

Hannah's story is written in the language of longing. It is shaped by quiet tears, unanswered prayers, and a faith that refuses to harden even when hope feels delayed. She is not a woman of public power or political influence. She is a wife, a worshiper, and a woman carrying a grief that speaks louder than words. And yet, through Hannah, God shifts the course of Israel's spiritual history.

Hannah lives in a divided household. She is married to Elkanah, a man who loves her deeply but cannot give her what she wants most—a child. In a time when motherhood was closely tied to identity, legacy, and security, Hannah's barrenness is not merely biological; it is social, emotional, and spiritual. Every year, she walks into worship carrying an invisible wound.

Her rival, Peninnah, bears children easily and uses that fruitfulness as a weapon. Peninnah provokes Hannah relentlessly, reminding her again and again of what her body has not produced. Scripture does not soften this cruelty. It names it plainly. Hannah is mocked in the very place she should feel safe—within her own household.

Elkanah tries to comfort her. He gives her a double portion. He asks, *"Am I not better to you than ten sons?"* His love is sincere—but love cannot always heal what only God can fill. Hannah's pain is not ingratitude. It is grief. And grief has its own language.

A Woman in Agony

Prayer Born From Pain

Hannah's sorrow follows her into the house of the Lord. At Shiloh, where Israel gathers to worship, Hannah does something radical: she brings her pain directly to God without performance. She weeps bitterly. Her lips move, but her voice does not rise. Her prayer is so raw, so unfiltered, that the priest Eli mistakes it for drunkenness.

This moment reveals Hannah's depth. She does not defend herself with anger. She explains herself with honesty. *"I am a woman of a sorrowful spirit,"* she says. In that sentence, Hannah gives voice to generations of women who have carried silent pain into sacred spaces.

Hannah makes a vow—not out of bargaining, but out of surrender. She promises that if God gives her a son, she will give him back. Not just symbolically, but completely. Her vow is costly. She is not asking for a child to fill her emptiness; she is asking for a child she is willing to release into God's service.

This is the turning point of her life. Scripture says that after she prayed, her countenance changed. Nothing had happened yet—but something shifted within her. Faith had replaced despair.

God Remembers Hannah

When Heaven Responds

God answers Hannah's prayer. She conceives and bears a son, naming him Samuel—"asked of God." Every time she speaks his name, she remembers where he came from. Samuel is not a trophy. He is testimony.

Hannah keeps her vow. When Samuel is still young, she brings him to the house of the Lord and leaves him there. This is not abandonment. It is obedience. She releases the very thing she prayed for, trusting that what is given to God is never truly lost.

Her faithfulness does not end with surrender—it deepens. Hannah returns year after year, bringing Samuel a little coat, stitching love into every thread. She mothers him from a distance, proving that motherhood is not diminished by obedience. It is expanded.

The Song of a Redeemed Woman

Praise That Shapes a Nation

Hannah does not leave Shiloh empty-handed or silent-hearted. She sings. Her song is one of the most powerful prayers in Scripture—bold, prophetic, and revolutionary. She praises a God who lifts the lowly and humbles the proud, who feeds the hungry and brings down the mighty.

Her song reaches beyond her personal victory. It becomes a spiritual framework for Israel's future. Centuries later, its echoes will be heard again in Mary's Magnificat. Hannah's private agony produces public theology.

God honors her faithfulness further. Hannah bears more children—sons and daughters—proving that God is not limited by what once seemed closed. But Samuel remains unique. He is the child of tears, prayer, and promise.

Hannah's Legacy

The Mother Who Changed the Course of Israel

Samuel grows into a prophet, judge, and kingmaker. He anoints Saul and David. He ushers Israel from a period of spiritual confusion into prophetic clarity. None of this happens without Hannah.

Hannah does not stand beside Samuel when he confronts kings. She does not speak publicly in his ministry. But her obedience undergirds his authority. Her faith creates space for his calling. Hannah's legacy is not built on visibility—it is built on surrender.

Why Hannah Matters

Faith That Refuses to Break

Hannah matters because she shows us how to pray when words fail. How to worship when mocked. How to wait when longing aches. She teaches that God is not offended by tears, that vows made in sincerity matter, and that faithfulness includes keeping your word even when it costs you deeply.

She reminds us that barrenness does not mean absence of favor. That silence does not mean rejection. That God remembers women who pour out their souls before Him.

Hannah's life declares a holy truth:
pain can become prayer,
prayer can become promise,
and promise—when surrendered—can shape nations.

She was mocked,
she was barren,
she was brokenhearted.

And she became the mother of a prophet.

Hannah still speaks to women who are waiting, praying, aching, and believing. Her story assures us that God hears the prayers whispered through tears—and that faith, when trusted fully, can bring forth something greater than we ever imagined.

A Message from Hannah

I speak to you as a woman who learned how to pray when words could no longer carry the weight of her longing. I speak from the place where tears fall before sound, where the heart speaks louder than the mouth ever could. If you are waiting for something that feels delayed beyond reason, sit with me for a moment. I know that ache.

I prayed from pain, not from performance. I did not dress my grief in polite language or hide my sorrow behind strong smiles. I poured my soul out before the Most High and trusted that He could hold what others misunderstood. When they thought I was weak, God knew I was faithful. When they misjudged my silence, Heaven heard every word.

Believe even when your circumstances argue against you. Faith is not pretending the pain is gone—it is choosing to trust God while the pain is still present. I walked away from the altar before I was pregnant, but I walked away changed. Peace met me before fulfillment ever did. That is how you know God has heard you.

And hear me clearly: when God answers your prayer, honor Him with your obedience. I vowed to give my son back, and I kept my word. Love does not break vows when fulfillment arrives—it strengthens them. Let your yes remain yes, even when surrender costs more than you expected.

I raised my son knowing he did not belong to me alone. I nurtured him, taught him, prayed over him—and then I released him into God's hands. I did not cling to him out of fear. I trusted that what is dedicated to God is safer than what is kept for ourselves. True motherhood is not possession—it is preparation.

Do not be afraid to give God what you waited for. He is not threatened by your obedience. He multiplies it. My faithfulness did not leave me empty—it expanded me. God gave me more than I asked for, but Samuel was always first in my heart, because he was born of prayer and shaped by promise.

I am Hannah.
I prayed when hope felt thin.
I believed when others misunderstood.
I kept my vow when fulfillment arrived.

Pray honestly.
Believe deeply.
Surrender faithfully.

God hears the prayers that are whispered through tears—and He is faithful to bring forth purpose from them.

Lessons I will Take from Hannah

_____

_____

_____

_____

_____

_____

_____

_____

_____

Chapter 12: Deborah

The Woman Who Heard God Clearly—and Taught a Nation to Rise

Deborah's life stands like a pillar in the middle of Israel's history—steady, unshakeable, and unmistakably authoritative. She does not arrive in Scripture asking permission to lead. She is already leading when we meet her. Already listening. Already discerning. Already trusted. In a time when Israel drifts, hesitates, and forgets its covenant identity, Deborah becomes both compass and conscience—a woman who hears God clearly and refuses to soften His word for comfort's sake.

She lives in an era of cycles: Israel strays, oppression follows, the people cry out, and God raises a deliverer. But Deborah is different from those who came before her. She is not merely a warrior or a rescuer. She is a prophetess and a judge—one who speaks the word of the Lord and interprets it with wisdom, applying heaven's truth to earthly decisions. She does not govern from a throne or a battlefield. She sits beneath a palm tree, and the people come to her.

That detail matters.

Deborah does not chase authority. Authority finds her because wisdom dwells with her. Men and women, elders and warriors, bring their disputes, fears, and questions to Deborah because they trust her discernment. She listens carefully, weighs matters justly, and speaks with clarity. Her leadership is not loud, but it is firm. Not aggressive, but undeniable.

A Prophetess With a Burden

Hearing God When the Nation Is Quiet

Deborah's first calling is not military—it is prophetic. She hears what God is saying to Israel when others have stopped listening. She knows when silence has gone on too long, when fear has settled into habit, when compromise has begun to feel normal. As a prophetess, she does not simply predict events—she calls the people back to covenant responsibility.

Israel is oppressed by Canaan under King Jabin, whose commander Sisera wields iron chariots—symbols of technological and military dominance. The people are intimidated, immobilized, worn down by years of subjugation. Deborah understands that the battle Israel faces is not merely political; it is spiritual. Fear has replaced faith.

So Deborah sends for Barak.

She delivers God's instruction plainly: gather men, go to Mount Tabor, and confront Sisera. There is no hesitation in her voice. No ambiguity. Deborah does not negotiate with fear. She speaks the word of the Lord as command, not suggestion.

Barak hesitates.

His response reveals the state of the nation's courage: *If you go with me, I will go. But if you do not go with me, I will not go.* It is not cowardice alone—it is dependence. He recognizes Deborah's spiritual authority and does not trust himself to move without it.

Deborah agrees to go, but she speaks truth without flattery. She tells Barak that the honor of victory will not be his—that God will deliver Sisera into the hands of a woman. Deborah is not offended by Barak's weakness, but she does not excuse it either. Leadership, in her hands, is honest.

Wisdom That Mobilizes Action

When Discernment Meets Courage

Deborah does not merely prophesy—she mobilizes. She understands timing. She knows when instruction must turn into movement. When the day of battle arrives, Deborah does not stand behind the lines. She stands in faith and declares, *"Up! For this is the day in which the Lord has delivered Sisera into your hand."*

Her confidence ignites courage.

The battle unfolds not by Israel's strength, but by God's intervention. Sisera's chariots become useless in the terrain God chooses. The mighty commander flees on foot and meets his end not by sword, but by the hand of another woman—Jael—fulfilling Deborah's prophecy exactly as spoken.

Deborah's discernment proves precise. God's word, delivered through her, stands unbroken.

A Leader Who Gives God the Glory

The Song That Interprets Victory

After the victory, Deborah does something rare and powerful: she sings. Alongside Barak, she composes a song—not to exalt herself, but to interpret the moment spiritually. The Song of Deborah is one of the oldest poems in Scripture, and it does more than celebrate triumph. It teaches the people how to understand what just happened.

She praises God.

She honors those who stepped forward willingly.

She rebukes tribes who stayed silent.

She names courage and calls out complacency.

Deborah understands that victory without reflection is temporary. Her song becomes theology set to rhythm—a reminder that deliverance comes when people answer God's call, and oppression lingers when they do not.

She does not hoard praise. She distributes it rightly. Leadership, for Deborah, means helping a nation remember who God is and who they are called to be.

Why Deborah Matters

Authority Rooted in Obedience

Deborah matters because she dismantles false ideas about leadership. She does not lead because she fights; she fights because she leads. Her authority is not derived from dominance, but from obedience. She does not compete with men; she complements the call of God by fulfilling her own.

She shows us that wisdom earns trust, that discernment creates stability, and that hearing God clearly is the foundation of all effective leadership. Deborah's life proves that when God speaks through a woman, nations move.

She was a counselor before she was a commander.
A prophetess before she was a judge.
A worshiper before she was a strategist.

Deborah teaches that leadership is not about position—it is about clarity. About courage. About responding when God speaks and refusing to let fear silence obedience.

She stands in Scripture as a reminder that God raises voices in every generation who will not soften truth, who will not delay obedience, and who will not shrink back when responsibility calls.

Deborah heard God.
Deborah spoke God's word.
And a nation found its courage again.

A Message from Deborah

Woman, listen to me.

I have watched people drift—not all at once, but little by little. I have seen hearts grow dull where they once burned. I have seen fear replace obedience, comfort replace conviction, opinion replace commandment. Do not pretend you do not see it. You see it. God has allowed you to see because He intends for you to *speak*.

Do not shrink back from that responsibility.

When Israel fell, it was not because God stopped speaking. It was because the people stopped listening. They traded His laws for convenience and His commandments for compromise. And still—God raised voices. He always does. I was one of them. You may be one now.

Talk to them. Not with arrogance. Not with contempt. But with clarity. Call people back to God's laws and commandments—

not as burden, but as protection. The law was never meant to crush us; it was meant to keep us whole. When people abandon it, chaos follows. When they return to it, life steadies.

Stay true to Christ. He did not come to erase obedience—He came to fulfill it and write it on the heart. Do not let anyone tell you that grace excuses disobedience. Grace empowers righteousness. Christ walked in perfect alignment with the Father, and He calls His people to walk as He walked.

You will encounter hesitation. You will meet resistance. You may even be told to soften your words. Do not. Truth spoken in love does not need dilution. When I spoke, I did not ask if the people were comfortable—I asked if they were ready to obey. Comfort does not save nations. Obedience does.

Lead where you are planted. Counsel when wisdom is sought. Warn when danger approaches. Encourage the willing and confront the fearful. Some will hesitate like Barak did—do not despise them, but do not allow their hesitation to delay God's timing either. Move when God says move.

And remember this: leadership does not always shout. Sometimes it sits beneath a tree and listens. Sometimes it waits for the right moment and then speaks one sentence that changes everything. Be that woman.

I am Deborah.
I saw the fall before the battle.
I spoke when silence would have kept people bound.

So speak.
Stand.
Stay faithful.

God still raises women who hear Him clearly—and when they do, people find their way back.

Lessons I will Take from Deborah

_____

_____

_____

_____

_____

_____

_____

_____

_____

Chapter 13: Huldah

The Woman Whose Words Weighed
More Than Crowns

Huldah's life unfolds quietly, but when her voice enters the record of Scripture, it carries the weight of heaven. She is not introduced in the midst of spectacle or public procession. She lives in Jerusalem, in a time when the nation's faith has grown brittle from neglect, when God's law has been forgotten so thoroughly that its rediscovery shocks the king himself. Huldah does not rise through ambition or rebellion. She stands already established—recognized, trusted, and sought out when truth matters most.

She is a prophetess in an age of reform, and that timing is not accidental.

Israel has drifted far from covenant faithfulness. Idolatry has been normalized. Sacred spaces have been defiled. Generations have lived without reference to the commandments that once defined them. And then, during the reign of Josiah—a young king with a tender conscience—the Book of the Law is found in the temple.

The discovery is devastating.

When the words of the Law are read aloud, Josiah tears his clothes in grief. He understands immediately what the nation has ignored: judgment is not coming because God is cruel, but because the people have been unfaithful. The king does not dismiss the text. He does not soften it. He does not seek prophets who will tell him what he wants to hear.

Instead, he seeks truth.

A Prophetess Sought in a Critical Hour

Wisdom That Kings Trust

Josiah sends a delegation to consult the Lord—and the people he chooses speak volumes. He sends the high priest Hilkiah, along with royal officials and scribes. These are powerful men, educated in temple protocol and state affairs. And yet, they do not go to another king. They do not go to military counsel. They go to a woman.

They go to Huldah.

This choice is not controversial in the narrative—it is natural. Huldah's authority is already recognized. Her reputation for wisdom and spiritual clarity is settled. When Scripture names her, it does not explain *why* she is trusted; it assumes it. That assumption tells us something profound: Huldah's life has been consistent, her discernment proven, her voice aligned with God long before this moment arrives.

She lives in the Second Quarter of Jerusalem, near the heart of the city, positioned close enough to power to be accessible—but not absorbed by it. She is married, rooted, and established, yet her identity is not derived from her household. She is identified by her calling.

The Word of the Lord, Unfiltered

Truth Without Flattery

When the delegation arrives, Huldah does not hesitate. She does not consult others. She does not soften the message to protect feelings or preserve favor. She speaks the word of the Lord directly, clearly, and without apology.

Judgment is coming.

She confirms what Josiah fears: the curses written in the Law will fall upon Judah because the people have forsaken God, burned incense to other gods, and provoked Him through their disobedience. Huldah does not dilute the message. She does not excuse generations of neglect. Her prophecy is firm, righteous, and precise.

But Huldah's discernment is not only severe—it is nuanced.

She also speaks mercy.

Because Josiah's heart was tender, because he humbled himself, tore his garments, and wept before the Lord, judgment will not come in his lifetime. He will be gathered to his grave in peace. Huldah recognizes repentance when she sees it. She distinguishes between national consequence and personal faithfulness. This balance reveals her spiritual maturity. She understands that God's justice does not cancel His compassion.

Huldah's prophecy gives Josiah both warning and direction. It does not paralyze him—it propels him.

A Word That Sparks Reform

When Prophecy Leads to Obedience

Josiah does not ignore Huldah's words. He responds with decisive reform. He gathers the people, reads the Law aloud, renews the covenant, destroys idols, purges the land, and re-centers worship on the commandments of God. One woman's obedience to speak truth becomes the catalyst for one of the greatest spiritual renewals in Judah's history.

Huldah does not stand in the spotlight of reform. She does not lead the procession. She does not claim credit. Her role is complete once the word is delivered. This is the mark of a true prophet: faithfulness to the message, not attachment to the outcome.

Why Huldah Matters

The Authority of Quiet Faithfulness

Huldah matters because she reveals what spiritual authority truly looks like. It is not volume. It is not position. It is not proximity to power. It is alignment with God. When leaders needed truth, they did not look for popularity—they looked for accuracy. And they found it in Huldah.

She reminds us that God entrusts His word to those who will carry it without distortion. That women are not sidelined in moments of national consequence. That wisdom cultivated in quiet faithfulness becomes indispensable when crisis comes.

Huldah did not shout from the streets.
She did not rally crowds.
She spoke once—and a nation changed course.

Her life teaches

A Message from Huldah

I speak as a woman who did not raise her voice to be heard, yet kings came to my door. I was not crowned, not carried into courts, not placed on a platform. I lived among ordinary walls, and God placed extraordinary truth in my mouth. Let that teach you this first lesson: authority does not require permission from people when it is appointed by God.

Do not shrink your discernment to make others comfortable. When the word of the Lord came to me, it was not gentle flattery. It was truth—clear, weighty, unavoidable. I did not soften it to spare pride. I did not delay it to protect reputation. I spoke what God said, exactly as He said it. Truth does not become holy because it is pleasant. It becomes holy because it is faithful.

Learn to sit with God before you speak for Him. I did not guess. I did not assume. I listened. Too many voices speak loudly today without ever bowing low. Wisdom is not volume. Wisdom is accuracy. And accuracy comes from reverence. When you fear God, you do not fear backlash.

Know this also: your gender does not disqualify your calling. I was a woman, and yet the word of God rested on me. Men with titles sought my counsel because God had chosen my voice. Do not allow anyone to tell you that humility requires silence. Humility requires obedience. And sometimes obedience requires speech.

Speak truth even when it announces consequences. I told a king that judgment was coming. I told him repentance mattered, but it would not erase what had already been sown. Compassion does not mean dishonesty. Love does not mean denial. A woman of God must learn to hold mercy in one hand and truth in the other—without dropping either.

Guard the Scriptures. When the Book of the Law was found, it was not a relic—it was a mirror. It revealed how far the people had drifted. The Word still does that. Return to it. Read it. Tremble at it. Do not reshape it to fit the times. Let it reshape you. Revival begins not with emotion, but with alignment.

And remember this: obscurity is not absence. I did not stand in the temple courts, yet heaven knew my address. If God has hidden you, it may be because He is preserving clarity. When the time comes, He knows exactly where to find you.

I am Huldah.
I listened before I spoke.

I spoke without fear.
I honored God above comfort.

Do the same.

Lessons I will Take from Huldah

_____

_____

_____

_____

_____

_____

_____

_____

_____

Chapter 14: Queen Esther

The Woman Who Used Her Position—and Risked

Her Life—for Her People

Esther's story begins quietly, almost invisibly, the way many lives of destiny do. She is a young Israelite woman living in exile, raised far from Jerusalem, shaped by survival more than ceremony. Her Hebrew name is Hadassah, but the world knows her as Esther—a name that allows her to move safely within a Persian empire that does not look kindly on her people. She is an orphan, raised by her cousin Mordecai, a man who teaches her wisdom, restraint, and reverence long before she ever understands how deeply she will need them.

Esther does not begin as a warrior. She begins as a listener. She watches how power works from the margins. She learns when to speak and when to stay silent. These early lessons are not accidental—they are preparation. Destiny often trains us quietly before it ever calls us publicly.

When King Ahasuerus removes Queen Vashti, Esther is drawn into a process she did not seek. She does not campaign for influence. She does not announce ambition. She is chosen. Scripture notes her beauty, but it is clear that her favor reaches deeper than appearance. Esther listens to counsel. She follows instruction. She walks with humility even as the crown is placed upon her head.

And yet, even as queen, Esther remains hidden. Her identity as an Israelite is concealed. Her position is elevated, but her people are still vulnerable. Esther lives in the tension many women know well—blessed personally while the community she loves remains endangered.

The Crisis

When Silence Becomes a Choice

The danger arrives in the form of Haman, a man whose pride metastasizes into hatred. Offended by Mordecai's refusal to bow, Haman plots not just revenge against one man, but genocide against an entire people. A decree is signed. The date is set. Death becomes policy.

Mordecai sends word to Esther, and the moment of her life arrives—not with applause, but with pressure. Esther hesitates. Approaching the king without invitation is punishable by death. Her fear is real. Her position does not make her immune.

Mordecai's response becomes one of the most piercing challenges in Scripture: *"Do not think that you will escape in the king's house more than all the Jews... And who knows whether you have come to the kingdom for such a time as this?"*

In that moment, Esther understands something profound: safety is an illusion when injustice is law. Silence is not neutrality—it is a decision.

Courage That Counts the Cost

"If I Perish, I Perish"

Esther does not rush forward recklessly. She fasts. She calls for the community to fast with her. Courage, for Esther, is not bravado—it is submission to God before confrontation with power. She prepares her spirit before she risks her body.

When she enters the king's presence uninvited, the moment stretches between life and death. The king extends his scepter.

Favor meets obedience. Esther lives—but she does not speak immediately. Her wisdom reveals itself again. She understands timing. She invites the king and Haman to a banquet. Then another. Esther allows tension to ripen before truth is revealed.

When she finally speaks, she does not accuse broadly. She testifies personally. She identifies with her people openly for the first time. She names the threat. She exposes the enemy. Her words pierce through palace politics and reach the king's conscience.

Haman falls. The decree is reversed. The Israelite people are allowed to defend themselves. Mourning turns to celebration. What was meant for destruction becomes deliverance.

Influence Used Righteously

Power With Purpose

Esther's greatness is not that she became queen—it is that she understood why she became queen. She does not hoard influence. She spends it. She risks comfort to protect covenant. Her courage saves a nation.

From this deliverance comes the festival of Purim, a lasting memorial to joy born from danger, light born from threat, and survival born from courage. Purim is not a quiet remembrance—it is loud, communal, celebratory. It honors the truth that God can work even when His name is not spoken aloud, even when His people are scattered, even when deliverance arrives through a woman standing in a palace she did not choose.

Why Esther Matters

Position Is Never Accidental

Esther matters because she shows us that influence is responsibility. That beauty, access, and favor are not rewards to be enjoyed privately but tools meant to be used publicly. She teaches that courage does not mean absence of fear—it means obedience in spite of it.

She reminds women today that where you stand matters. That your job, your platform, your voice, your access may not be for your comfort alone. That God often places people strategically before they understand the assignment.

Esther's life tells us this enduring truth:
deliverance often waits on courage,
courage often waits on obedience,
and obedience often begins with a woman willing to say, *"If I perish, I perish."*

She was an orphan.
She became a queen.
She saved her people.

And every year, when Purim is celebrated, Esther's legacy still speaks—declaring that faith, wisdom, and bravery can overturn even the most powerful systems of injustice.

Queen Esther did not seek the crown.
But when the moment came, she wore it for others.

A Message from Queen Esther

Queens—listen to me.

I did not always wear a crown. Before the palace, there was loss. Before the throne, there was hiding. I learned early how to survive quietly in a world that did not ask whether my people deserved to live. So when I speak to you now, understand this: courage is not something you suddenly find when danger arrives. It is something you build long before you are tested.

Be brave. Not reckless—but resolved. Fear will visit you. It visited me. I stood outside the king's chamber knowing one step forward could cost my life. Courage is not the absence of fear; it is the refusal to let fear decide for you. When persecution rises, neutrality becomes a luxury you no longer have. Silence does not keep you safe—it only delays the cost.

Use your influence. Every door that opened for you opened *on purpose*. Your position is not accidental. Your access is not random. Your voice is not decoration. Whether you sit in boardrooms, classrooms, courtrooms, kitchens, or community spaces—what you carry matters. Influence unused is influence wasted. And wasted influence leaves people unprotected.

Fight for your people. Not with hatred. Not with vengeance. But with clarity, wisdom, and timing. I did not rush my words. I fasted. I prayed. I listened. Then I spoke when the moment could no longer be postponed. Learn the power of timing. Learn the strength of preparation. Learn when to speak softly—and when to speak plainly.

Do not underestimate how dangerous injustice becomes when it is legalized. I watched genocide turn into policy. I learned that evil often wears official signatures and polite language. When you see systems designed to erase, diminish, or criminalize your people—stand up. Even if your knees shake. Even if your voice trembles. Heaven honors risk taken for righteousness.

And remember this, queens: you were not crowned to be comfortable. You were crowned to be courageous. The crown is not for display—it is for responsibility. If I had protected my own safety and abandoned my people, history would have remembered my silence, not my name.

I am Esther.
I fasted before I fought.
I risked my life so others could live.

So rise, queens.
Be strategic.
Be faithful.
Be fearless when it counts.

If you have been placed where you are, *now*, in this moment—
it is not coincidence.
It is calling.

Lessons I will Take from Queen Esther

_____

_____

_____

_____

_____

_____

_____

_____

_____

Chapter 15: Elizabeth

The Woman Who Waited Faithfully—and Was
Remembered by God

Elizabeth's life is shaped by devotion long before it is touched by miracle. She is not introduced as extraordinary by circumstance, but as faithful by character. Scripture describes her and her husband, Zechariah, as *righteous before God, walking blamelessly in all the commandments and ordinances*

of the Lord. That description is not casual—it is deliberate. It places Elizabeth among those rare souls whose faith is not seasonal, not performative, and not dependent on reward.

Yet Elizabeth carries a grief that devotion alone has not relieved. She is barren. And not young-barren, where hope still feels close enough to touch, but *aged*—past the season where expectation is socially acceptable. In a culture where fruitfulness was often mistaken for favor, Elizabeth bears the quiet weight of misunderstanding. People see her obedience, but they also see her empty arms. They assume what they always assume: if God had wanted to bless her, surely He would have done it by now.

Elizabeth does not argue with them. She does not defend herself. She lives her faith out loud without demanding explanation.

Blameless, Yet Waiting

Faith That Refuses to Sour

Elizabeth's righteousness is not transactional. She does not obey God to earn a miracle. She obeys because He is worthy. This distinction matters deeply. Many walk faithfully while secretly keeping score—serving with expectation, worshiping with conditions. Elizabeth does not. Her trust is unwavering, not because life has been easy, but because God has been consistent.

Together, Elizabeth and Zechariah keep the commandments. They keep the rhythms of prayer, service, and sacrifice. Zechariah serves in the temple as a priest; Elizabeth serves in the home and community with the same reverence. Their marriage is marked by unity of purpose—a shared commitment to God's law, not to reputation.

Still, the years pass. Silence lingers. The ache does not leave.

And then, in God's timing—not theirs—heaven interrupts.

God Remembers

When Waiting Meets Fulfillment

While Zechariah serves in the temple, an angel appears and announces what once seemed impossible: Elizabeth will conceive and bear a son. The angel does not frame this child as a consolation prize for long waiting. He frames him as a turning point for Israel. This child will be great before the Lord. He will prepare the way. He will be filled with the Holy Spirit *even from the womb*.

When Elizabeth conceives, her response is not boastful—it is worshipful. She withdraws for a season, letting the miracle settle into her spirit. Her words reveal the depth of her humility: *"Thus hath the Lord dealt with me, in the days wherein he looked on me, to take away my reproach among men."*

Elizabeth understands something profound: the reproach was never God's judgment—it was human misunderstanding. God did not correct Himself by blessing her. He revealed Himself.

A Womb Filled With the Spirit

Holiness Before Birth

Elizabeth's pregnancy is not ordinary. Scripture tells us that her child, John the Baptist, is filled with the Holy Spirit from the womb. This detail is extraordinary. Before John ever preaches repentance, before he ever cries out in the wilderness, his life is already consecrated. Elizabeth becomes the first dwelling place of a prophet whose voice will shake a nation.

When Mary visits Elizabeth, carrying the Messiah in her own womb, something holy happens. John leaps. Elizabeth is filled with the Holy Spirit. And she speaks—not from emotion, but from revelation. She recognizes Mary's child before the world ever will. Elizabeth's discernment, sharpened by years of faithfulness, allows her to see what others cannot yet perceive.

Her voice becomes prophetic praise: *"Blessed art thou among women."* Elizabeth does not envy Mary's youth or calling. She celebrates it. She understands that God's work is not competitive—it is cooperative.

Motherhood Without Idolatry

Raising a Son Who Belonged to God

Elizabeth becomes a mother late in life, but she does not clutch her son in fear of losing him. She understands that John belongs to God before he belongs to her. When neighbors and family attempt to name the child according to tradition, Elizabeth insists on obedience: his name is John. She honors the word of the Lord even when it disrupts expectation.

Her motherhood is purposeful, not possessive. She nurtures John in holiness, preparing him for a life that will not be comfortable or celebrated. She raises a son who will live in the wilderness, speak truth to power, and ultimately lose his life for righteousness. Elizabeth's faith does not end with conception—it extends into release.

Why Elizabeth Matters

Faithfulness That Outlasts Delay

Elizabeth matters because she shows us what enduring righteousness looks like. She teaches that obedience is not invalidated by delay, that barrenness does not negate favor, and that God's promises are not constrained by time.

She is a woman who kept the commandments when no one was watching closely. Who honored God without guarantee. Who waited without bitterness. Who recognized Messiah before the crowds ever did. Who raised a son not for her own fulfillment, but for God's purpose.

Elizabeth's life tells us this enduring truth:
God does not forget the faithful.
He remembers them at the right time.

She waited.
She trusted.
She obeyed.

And when God moved, He moved decisively—filling her womb with a prophet and her mouth with praise.

Elizabeth stands as a witness to women everywhere: faithfulness is never wasted, obedience is never unseen, and God's promises arrive not when we are ready—but when *He* is.

A Message from Elizabeth

Daughter, come close and listen to me—not as one above you, but as one who walked a long road with God and learned how to stay faithful when faith felt costly.

Stay devout. Not loudly. Not performatively. Stay devout in the quiet choices no one applauds. Keep God's laws and commandments even when the world treats obedience like foolishness and compromise like wisdom. I lived righteously in a time when corruption blended easily into daily life. Sin did not disappear because I was faithful—but neither did God. Do not let the darkness of the age convince you to dim your devotion.

I obeyed God without knowing whether I would ever see the promise fulfilled. Years passed. My body aged. Hope grew thin. Still, I walked blamelessly—not because reward was guaranteed, but because God was worthy. Learn this: obedience is not a transaction. It is trust made visible.

Raise your children as if they could be the next prophet of Israel. Speak truth into them before the world teaches lies. Shape their character before culture shapes their appetite. Do not raise them for comfort—raise them for calling. My son was filled with the Holy Spirit before he ever took his first breath. That did not happen by accident. It happened because holiness was cultivated around him long before he could choose for himself.

Teach your children to fear God more than crowds. To love righteousness more than applause. To stand firm even when truth costs them something. They may not live ordinary lives—and that is not a failure. Some children are born for wilderness paths, for bold voices, for difficult assignments. Do not pull them back because the road looks lonely. Prepare them instead.

And stay true to Christ. Do not let anyone convince you that grace excuses disobedience. Grace empowers it. Christ did not call us away from holiness—He called us deeper into it. He fulfilled the law and wrote it on the heart so that obedience could live, not as burden, but as love expressed through action.

I was overlooked for years. Misunderstood. Quietly faithful in a world that measured worth by visible blessing. And then— God remembered me. Not because I demanded, but because He is faithful to those who remain faithful to Him.

I am Elizabeth.
I obeyed when nothing changed.
I waited when time said it was too late.
I raised a son who belonged to God before he belonged to me.

So stay devout, daughter.
Stay disciplined.
Stay holy.

The world may not notice your faithfulness—but heaven does.
And what God births through a devoted woman can change generations.

Lessons I will Take from Elizabeth

_____

_____

_____

_____

_____

_____

_____

_____

_____

Chapter 16: Mary (Mother of Jesus)

The Woman Who Said Yes When the World Would Not Understand

Mary's story begins in obscurity, not prominence. She is not introduced as royalty, scholar, or prophetess, but as a young woman in Nazareth—a place small enough to be dismissed, ordinary enough to be overlooked. Nothing in her environment suggests that history is about to bend around her obedience. And yet, God chooses her.

Not because she is loud.

Not because she is powerful.

But because she is humble, faithful, and available.

Mary lives a life ordered by devotion. She is betrothed to Joseph, committed to covenant before convenience, purity before impulse. In a culture where honor matters deeply and reputation can determine survival, Mary has learned discipline. She knows the weight of obedience. She understands what it costs to live rightly in a watching world.

And then heaven interrupts her ordinary life.

The Announcement

Faith Confronted With the Impossible

When the angel Gabriel appears, Mary is not flattered—she is troubled. Confused. Afraid. The greeting alone unsettles her. And when the message comes—that she will conceive and bear a son by the power of the Holy Spirit—Mary asks the most honest question a woman could ask: *How shall this be, seeing I know not a man?*

This question is not doubt. It is integrity.

Mary is chaste. She has not slept with Joseph. She has kept herself pure, obedient to God's law and faithful to her betrothal. Her life testifies to restraint, not recklessness. The miracle of the incarnation does not bypass holiness—it honors it.

When Gabriel explains that this conception will be divine, not human—that the Holy Spirit will overshadow her—Mary faces a decision no woman before her has faced. Saying yes will cost her safety. Her reputation. Possibly her life. Unwed pregnancy is not misunderstood in her culture—it is condemned.

Mary understands the weight immediately.

Yet she answers with words that echo through eternity: *"Behold the handmaid of the Lord; be it unto me according to thy word."*

This is not passive submission. This is courageous obedience.

Bearing the Weight

Faith Under Judgment

Mary carries the Messiah in a body that becomes subject to scrutiny, gossip, and suspicion. Whispers follow her steps. Eyes linger too long. Questions go unanswered. She cannot fully explain what God has done without sounding unbelievable. Faith, for Mary, means trusting God while being misunderstood by nearly everyone else.

Joseph himself struggles to understand until God intervenes. Even then, the road is not easy. Mary travels while pregnant. She gives birth away from home. There is no palace, no ceremony—only a manger and the quiet miracle of God made flesh.

Mary's obedience does not protect her from hardship. It carries her through it.

A Humble Witness

Faith That Ponders

Mary does not center herself in the story of redemption. She treasures things quietly. She ponders them in her heart. She listens more than she speaks. Even when shepherds and wise men arrive, even when prophecies surround her child, Mary remains grounded.

She raises Jesus Christ not as a spectacle, but as a son. She feeds Him. Teaches Him. Watches Him grow. She does not rush His calling. She trusts God's timing. At Cana, she does not demand a miracle—she simply presents the need and leaves the outcome to Him.

Mary's faith matures from astonishment to endurance. She follows Jesus not just through miracles, but through rejection. And ultimately, she stands at the cross—bearing a grief no mother should have to carry. The same body that once carried the Savior now stands powerless to save Him from suffering.

Still, she does not turn away.

Chosen, Yet Human

Obedience Without Illusion

Mary is not elevated because she is flawless. She is elevated because she is faithful. She feels fear. She feels confusion. She feels sorrow. But she never allows those emotions to override obedience.

Her chastity matters. Her purity matters. Her restraint matters. God does not ignore holiness when He performs miracles—He builds upon it. Mary's womb becomes holy ground because her life was already set apart.

Why Mary Matters

The Courage to Say Yes

Mary matters because she shows us what true faith looks like when it costs everything. She reminds us that obedience is not glamorous. That holiness may invite misunderstanding. That saying yes to God may mean standing alone.

She teaches women that purity is powerful. That humility is strength. That obedience does not require full understanding—only trust.

Mary's life declares this truth clearly:
God does not look for the loudest voice.
He looks for the willing heart.

She was young.
She was faithful.
She was afraid.
And she said yes anyway.

And through her obedience, salvation entered the world.

Mary did not choose comfort.
She chose calling.

And because she did, the Word became flesh—and dwelt among us.

A Message from Mary

Daughter, let me speak to you from the place where calling first met fear.

There will be moments when God asks something of you that no one around you will understand. Your story will sound impossible. Your obedience will look suspicious. Your faith will be questioned by people who believe only what they can explain. I lived there. I carried a miracle that could not be proven, only trusted.

Society did not believe my story. They saw my body before they listened to my God. They judged what they could see and dismissed what they could not comprehend. And yet, heaven knew the truth. Learn this early: the approval of people is fragile, but the assignment of God is eternal. Stay true to God's mission over your life, even when no one claps for your obedience.

I was afraid—but I did not let fear decide for me. I was confused—but I did not let confusion cancel my calling. Faith does not mean you understand everything. Faith means you say yes while your hands tremble and your heart races. When God speaks, obedience matters more than explanation.

Guard your purity. I kept myself until marriage, not because it was easy, but because holiness prepares you for purpose. Purity is not punishment—it is protection. It is the quiet strength that allows God to entrust you with weighty things. Do not let the world convince you that restraint is weakness. God builds His greatest works on lives that are set apart.

People may whisper. They may misunderstand your choices. They may accuse what they cannot control. Let them talk. You are not called to be believable—you are called to be faithful. God will defend what He authors.

Treasure what God places within you. Not every promise needs to be announced. Some things grow best in silence, prayer, and patience. I pondered much in my heart before I ever spoke. Learn when to hold things close and when to release them in God's time.

And hear this: obedience will carry you through joy *and* sorrow. Saying yes to God does not spare you from pain—but it anchors you when pain comes. I followed my Son from the manger to the cross. Faith held me when nothing else could.

I am Mary.

I said yes without knowing how.

I trusted God when the world doubted me.

I stayed pure so His purpose could dwell within me.

So stand firm, daughter.

Stay obedient.

Stay holy.

Even if no one believes your story—God does. And His word over your life will not return void.

Lessons I will Take from the Virgin Mary

Chapter 17: Mary Magdalene

The Woman Who Was Restored—and Refused to Leave

Mary Magdalene's life is a testimony to the mercy of God and the danger of human misunderstanding. She enters the story of Scripture already burdened by labels, already reduced by assumption, already carrying a past others believe defines her. But Jesus never meets her where people left her. He meets her where she truly is—and everything changes.

Mary comes from Magdala, a town known for commerce and reputation, a place easily judged from a distance. Scripture tells us that Jesus cast seven demons out of her—not to shame her, but to reveal the depth of her deliverance. Her bondage was real. Her suffering was real. And her restoration would be undeniable. Jesus does not expose her to humiliate her; He heals her to restore her.

From that moment forward, Mary is not merely healed—she is devoted.

Forgiveness That Rebuilds a Life

When Mercy Becomes Identity

Mary's transformation is not quiet. It is complete. She does not return to her former life. She follows Jesus. She supports His ministry. She listens to His teaching. She walks the roads others walk only briefly. Forgiveness, for Mary, is not theoretical—it is embodied. She understands what it means to be given back your mind, your dignity, your selfhood.

Those who have been forgiven much often love deeply. Mary's faith is fierce because her freedom was costly. She does not debate Jesus' worthiness—she knows it personally. Where others follow out of curiosity, Mary follows out of gratitude. Her loyalty is not performative; it is persistent.

Misunderstood by the World

Faith That Endures Distortion

History has not always been kind to Mary Magdalene. Over time, her name becomes tangled in false narratives, sexualized assumptions, and careless interpretation. Scripture never calls her a prostitute. The text never diminishes her character. But the world often does what it always does to redeemed women—it rewrites their story to keep them small.

Mary lives with misunderstanding not only from strangers, but from tradition. Yet she never corrects her reputation. She lets her faith speak instead. She remains close to Jesus, not demanding validation, not seeking spotlight, but anchored in relationship.

A Disciple Who Stayed

Love That Did Not Flee

When Jesus is arrested, many disciples scatter. Fear breaks formation. But Mary stays.

She stands at the cross with other women, watching the One who healed her suffer publicly. She does not turn away from His pain. She does not retreat when hope appears crucified. Her faith does not depend on outcome—it depends on love.

Mary watches Him die. She watches Him buried. And when Sabbath ends, she returns—not for answers, but for devotion. She goes to the tomb expecting death, but willing to honor Him anyway. This is faith stripped of reward.

The First Witness

Chosen to Speak Resurrection

At the empty tomb, Mary weeps. Grief clouds her vision. She mistakes Jesus for a gardener—until He speaks her name.

"Mary."

In that single word, recognition explodes. Resurrection becomes personal. Jesus does not first appear to kings, priests, or scholars. He appears to a woman once delivered, often dismissed, deeply faithful. He entrusts her with the greatest announcement in human history.

Mary Magdalene becomes the first witness of the resurrection.

Jesus sends her to speak—to tell the disciples that He is alive. Her voice carries the turning point of eternity. The risen Christ chooses a woman the world misunderstood to proclaim the truth the world could not yet comprehend.

A Relationship Marked by Presence

Close, Faithful, Trusted

Mary's relationship with Jesus Christ is not romanticized—it is sacred. It is built on deliverance, trust, and presence. She follows Him not from obligation, but from love. She understands Him not as an idea, but as Savior.

Jesus honors her faith by trusting her voice. He does not silence her. He commissions her. In doing so, He overturns cultural expectations and affirms spiritual authority rooted in transformation.

Why Mary Magdalene Matters

The Power of Redemption Witnessed

Mary Magdalene matters because she embodies the truth that redemption redefines identity. She reminds us that being healed does not make you invisible—it makes you qualified. That faith born from deliverance often stands strongest when others flee.

She teaches us that misunderstanding does not cancel calling. That a past does not disqualify a future. That proximity to Jesus changes everything.

Mary was forgiven.
Mary was faithful.
Mary stayed.
Mary spoke.

And because she did, the world heard first from a woman once bound that death had been defeated.

Mary Magdalene stands in Scripture as a witness to the transforming power of Christ—a woman restored, trusted, and sent. Her life declares that Jesus does not choose messengers based on reputation, but on devotion.

She was not what people said she was.
She was who Jesus healed her to be.

And she still speaks—of forgiveness that frees, love that endures, and faith that recognizes resurrection even through tears.

A Message from Mary Magdalene

Let me say it plain—because I don't need my story cleaned up to make it holy.

I'm from the hood. Magdala. Galilee. Around the way. The part of town people side-eye and warn their kids about. The kind of place where survival teaches you lessons before peace ever gets a chance to. I wasn't raised with privilege. I was raised with pressure. I was in the world heavy—caught up in things I won't dress up with fancy words. I did what I did trying to live, trying to numb pain I didn't have language for yet.

Folks thought they knew me. They labeled me before they listened. Decided my value based on my past and my zip code. And truth be told, some days I believed them.

But then the Messiah came through my neighborhood.

Not the rich part. Not the respectable part. *My* part. He didn't flinch at my reputation. Didn't ask me to fix myself first. Didn't need me to sound religious or look polished. He saw the hood, the hurt, the chaos—and He still stopped for me.

And He loved me.

He cast the darkness out of me, yes—but more than that, He gave me my mind back. My dignity back. My future back. I wasn't just forgiven—I was *restored*. And when He healed me, I didn't go back to the old blocks, the old habits, the old chains. I followed Him. Everywhere.

When things got tense, I stayed.
When folks ran, I stood.
When hope looked dead, I came back anyway.

I stood at the cross when loving Him hurt. I went to the tomb when all I expected was grief. And He spoke my name—*my name*—like I was known before the world ever misnamed me. He trusted an around-the-way woman to be the first witness that death was defeated.

So hear me, sister from the hood, sister from the struggle:

Where you're from does not disqualify you.
What you've done does not define you.
What they say about you does not override what God says.

Jesus came to *me*.
A hood woman.

A woman with a past.
A woman folks wrote off.

And if He came for me—
He will come for you.

I'm Mary Magdalene.
From Magdala.
From the hood.
From the world.

And I was renewed.
I was trusted.
I was loved by the Messiah.

Lessons I will Take from the Mary Magdalene

_____

_____

_____

_____

_____

_____

_____

_____

Chapter 18: Martha

The Woman Who Learned That Faith Is More Than Service

Martha's life is shaped by devotion expressed through action. She is not distant from Jesus, not curious at arm's length, but deeply involved—opening her home, her table, and her daily rhythms to the Messiah. Martha lives in Bethany with her siblings, Mary of Bethany and Lazarus, and their household becomes a place of refuge for Jesus Christ. This is not casual hospitality. This is discipleship lived out through responsibility, order, and care.

Martha is a woman who shows love by doing. She prepares. She plans. She carries weight. In a world where women's labor often went unseen, Martha's work mattered—it sustained community and made space for ministry. Her faith is practical, embodied, and generous. She does not merely admire Jesus; she supports His mission with her life.

Yet Martha's story is also about tension—the tension between service and stillness, between responsibility and presence, between doing *for* God and being *with* Him.

Distracted by Good Things

When Service Slips Into Strain

When Jesus visits their home, Martha moves instinctively into action. Meals must be prepared. Guests must be cared for. Nothing should be neglected. Meanwhile, Mary sits at Jesus' feet, listening. This contrast becomes the defining moment by which Martha is often remembered—but that remembrance is frequently shallow.

Martha's frustration is not rooted in selfishness; it is rooted in responsibility. She feels the weight of expectation. She sees what must be done. And when Mary does not help, Martha voices her complaint—not to Mary, but to Jesus.

Her words reveal her struggle: *"Lord, dost thou not care that my sister hath left me to serve alone?"*

Jesus' response is gentle but corrective. He does not rebuke Martha's service; He reorders her priorities. He names her anxiety, her distraction, her burdened spirit. *"Martha, Martha, thou art careful and troubled about many things: but one thing is needful."*

This moment does not diminish Martha—it matures her. Jesus invites her to understand that spiritual attentiveness must come before spiritual labor. Service without presence can become noise. Work without worship can become weight.

Faith Under Pressure

Trust That Does Not Collapse in Grief

Martha's deepest expression of faith emerges not in the kitchen, but at the grave.

When Lazarus becomes ill, Martha and Mary send word to Jesus, confident He can heal their brother. This confidence is unshaken even when Jesus delays. But delay does not feel holy when death arrives. Lazarus dies, and grief overtakes the household.

When Jesus finally comes, Martha does not hide. She goes out to meet Him. Her words are honest, raw, and reverent: *"Lord, if thou hadst been here, my brother had not died."* This is not accusation—it is trust wrestling with disappointment.

And then Martha speaks one of the clearest declarations of faith in the Gospels: *"But I know, that even now, whatsoever thou wilt ask of God, God will give it thee."*

Martha believes beyond timing. She trusts Jesus beyond outcomes. When Jesus tells her that Lazarus will rise again, Martha affirms resurrection theology. But Jesus presses deeper, revealing Himself not merely as one who *brings* resurrection, but as Resurrection itself.

And Martha responds with conviction: *"Yea, Lord: I believe that thou art the Christ, the Son of God, which should come into the world."*

This is not the confession of a distracted servant. This is the testimony of a disciple.

Witness to Glory

From Frustration to Revelation

When Jesus commands the stone to be rolled away, Martha hesitates again—this time not from busyness, but from realism. Death is final. The body has been sealed. But Jesus calls her forward in faith once more: *"Said I not unto thee, that, if thou wouldest believe, thou shouldest see the glory of God?"*

And she does.

Martha watches her brother walk out of the grave. The woman once anxious about preparation becomes a witness to resurrection power. Her faith—tested, corrected, deepened—finds its fulfillment not in perfect understanding, but in trust.

Why Martha Matters

Faith That Learns to Listen

Martha matters because she represents believers who love God through responsibility and service. She speaks to women who carry households, ministries, families, and communities—and sometimes forget to sit still in God's presence.

Her story teaches that devotion expressed through action must be anchored in relationship. That frustration can be a signal, not a failure. That faith matures when it learns to listen.

Martha is not the woman who "got it wrong."
She is the woman who *grew*.

She served faithfully.
She spoke honestly.
She believed deeply.

And when it mattered most, she stood face to face with Jesus—not as a busy hostess, but as a woman who knew exactly who He was.

Martha's life reminds us that Christ does not reject our service—but He calls us first to Himself. When presence leads, service follows rightly. And faith, once refined, becomes a powerful witness to the glory of God.

A Message from Martha

Let me tell you my truth, sister—because it's closer to yours than you might think.

I served. With my hands, my time, my whole heart. I opened my home to Jesus. I made room for Him in the practical ways—the food, the order, the preparation that keeps life moving. I believed serving Him meant doing everything well, doing everything myself, doing everything *right*. And I loved Him through my work.

But I got frustrated.

I got tired. I felt unseen. I looked around and thought, *Why am I the only one carrying this?* I let comparison creep in. I let pressure turn into irritation. I loved Jesus, but I forgot to sit with Him. And in my frustration, I spoke—not out of disrespect, but out of exhaustion.

And He didn't shame me.

He called my name.
Twice.
Softly.

He showed me that service without presence can weigh the soul down. That doing good things can still distract you from the *best* thing. I learned that Jesus does not measure devotion by productivity. He measures it by proximity.

But hear this too—I had faith.

When my brother died, I did not collapse into despair. I went to Jesus with my grief, my questions, my disappointment—and my trust. I believed He could have healed. I believed He still held power. I believed even when I didn't understand His timing. I stood at the edge of the grave and declared who He was.

And I saw resurrection.

So if you are a woman who serves—know that Jesus sees you. If you are frustrated—bring it to Him, not away from Him. If you are tired—sit down at His feet before you burn out in His name.

And if your faith is being tested—hold on. Faith does not mean you never struggle. It means you keep showing up, even with questions in your mouth and hope in your chest.

I am Martha.
I served.

I got frustrated.
I believed anyway.

And Jesus met me in *all* of it.

Lessons I will Take from the Martha

_____

_____

_____

_____

_____

_____

_____

_____

Chapter 19: Mary of Bethany

The Woman Who Chose Presence—and Was Changed Forever

Mary of Bethany lives her life close to holy ground. Not because she travels widely or speaks loudly, but because she recognizes where God is present—and she stays there. While others measure faith by movement and accomplishment, Mary measures it by nearness. She is a disciple shaped not by urgency, but by attention. Her story teaches that transformation does not always come through doing more, but through being fully present with the One who gives life meaning.

Mary lives in Bethany with her siblings—Martha, whose faith is expressed through service, and Lazarus, whose life will later bear witness to resurrection power. Their home becomes a place where Jesus rests, teaches, and reveals Himself. And in that home, Mary makes a choice that will define her legacy.

Sitting at His Feet

Discipleship Without Apology

When Jesus enters the house, Mary sits at His feet. This is not a casual posture. In her culture, sitting at a rabbi's feet is the position of a disciple—a learner who intends to be shaped by what she hears. Mary crosses an unspoken line, not with rebellion, but with devotion. She claims space where wisdom is being poured out.

Her sister Martha is busy serving, carrying the weight of hospitality with faithful hands. Mary carries nothing but attention. And when Martha complains, Jesus does not dismiss service—but He defends Mary's choice. *"Mary hath chosen that good part, which shall not be taken away from her."*

In that moment, Jesus affirms a truth that still unsettles hurried hearts: presence is not laziness. Listening is not neglect. Worship is not a distraction from responsibility—it is the source that gives responsibility meaning.

Mary understands something others miss. She senses that moments with Jesus are not guaranteed. She receives His words as nourishment, storing them deep within. The power of her discipleship lies in her willingness to be still when stillness is costly.

Worship That Breaks Open the Heart

Love Poured Out Without Calculation

Later, Mary's devotion becomes visible in a way that startles everyone in the room. She brings costly ointment—pure nard—and pours it out on Jesus, wiping His feet with her hair. The fragrance fills the house. The moment interrupts conversation. The act invites criticism.

Others call it wasteful. Mary calls it worship.

She does not calculate the return on devotion. She does not measure love by efficiency. She gives extravagantly because she understands who stands before her. Mary's worship is prophetic—an unspoken recognition that Jesus' time is short, that His death is near, that honor must be given now, not later.

Jesus receives her offering and defends her again. He understands her intuition. Presence has taught her what productivity never could.

Presence That Prepares the Soul

Learning Before Understanding

Mary's life is shaped by listening long before it is shaped by clarity. She does not ask many questions in Scripture; she absorbs truth quietly. Her discipleship is not loud, but it is deep. When Lazarus dies, Mary grieves—falling at Jesus' feet again, this time in sorrow. Presence does not exempt her from pain. It anchors her within it.

Jesus weeps with her.

And then He raises Lazarus from the dead.

Mary's proximity to Jesus places her at the center of miracle, not because she demands it, but because she remains near. She learns that presence brings intimacy, intimacy brings understanding, and understanding brings peace—even when life breaks open.

Why Mary of Bethany Matters

The Transformative Power of Nearness

Mary of Bethany matters because she shows us that discipleship is relational before it is functional. She reminds us that listening shapes us in ways activity never can. That worship poured out in love is never wasted. That stillness is not spiritual weakness—it is spiritual strength.

She teaches women that it is holy to sit and listen, to receive before responding, to value presence over performance. In a world addicted to motion, Mary offers a quieter courage—the courage to remain.

Mary was not passive.
She was attentive.

She was not idle.
She was anchored.

She did not chase influence.
She chose presence—and found transformation there.

Mary of Bethany still speaks to every woman pulled in a thousand directions:
Sit down.
Listen closely.
Stay near.

Because when you encounter the presence of God—not as a concept, but as a Person—you are changed. And that change, once begun, can never be taken away.

A Message from Mary of Bethany

Sister, let me tell you what I learned by staying close.

I served too. Don't let anyone tell you I didn't. I knew the rhythms of a home, the quiet work that keeps love alive. I knew how to show care in ordinary ways. But there came a moment when I understood that service alone could not hold my soul together. There came a moment when Presence mattered more than productivity.

So I sat at the feet of the Messiah.

I chose stillness when noise felt safer. I chose listening when movement would have earned approval. I chose nearness when everyone else was busy proving devotion. Sitting there was not laziness—it was hunger. I needed His words more than I needed to be seen doing good things. I needed His voice to shape me from the inside out.

And faith grew there.

Faith grows when you listen long enough for truth to settle. Faith grows when you stop rushing God and start receiving Him. At His feet, I learned who He was—not as rumor, not as miracle-worker alone, but as Life itself. I learned that worship is not always loud. Sometimes it is quiet attention. Sometimes it is tears held back and breath held still.

I poured out what was costly because love taught me timing. I honored Him while He was still with us, not waiting for a safer moment that never comes. Presence will do that—it sharpens your discernment. It teaches you when to speak, when to give, when to remain silent and simply stay.

I had faith even when grief knocked me to the ground. When my brother died, I went back to His feet—again. Because that is where sorrow belongs. Jesus met me there. He wept with me there. And from that place of nearness, resurrection followed.

So hear me, woman of today:

Serve, yes—but do not let service replace intimacy. Sit—without apology, without hurry, without shame. Believe—that what you receive in His presence will carry you through what you cannot control.

I am Mary of Bethany.
I served.
I sat at the feet of the Messiah.
I believed.

And I learned that nothing—nothing—transforms a life like choosing to stay close to God when the world keeps telling you to rush past Him.

Lessons I will Take from the Mary of Bethany

_____

_____

_____

_____

_____

_____

_____

_____

_____

Chapter 20: The Traditions of Biblical Women

Across Scripture, from Eve forward, the women of God share a striking commonality that is often overlooked in modern retellings: they ordered their lives around the commandments of God, not the customs of surrounding nations. These women did not blend covenant obedience with cultural religion. They kept what God commanded, even while living among peoples saturated with pagan worship. From the first woman in Eden to the women who walked with Christ, obedience was not abstract—it shaped their households, calendars, worship, and identity. Sabbath rest was not optional. God's appointed times were not symbolic accessories. They were lived realities that structured daily life and generational faithfulness.

Queen Esther, Miriam, Elizabeth, Virgin Mary, and Mary Magdalene did not adopt the religious traditions of Persia, Egypt, Rome, or Greece. They did not replace God's feast days with the festivals of the Gentiles. They did not mark time by the sun gods, fertility cycles, or imperial celebrations. Instead, they kept Passover, the Sabbath, the New Moons, and the appointed feasts given to Israel—because these were not merely rituals; they were covenant markers. Even in exile, oppression, or Roman occupation, these women remained anchored to God's calendar, trusting that obedience—not assimilation—was preservation.

Today, Jesus' words in Mark 7:9 echo with clarity: *"Full well ye reject the commandment of God, that ye may keep your own tradition."* Many modern religious holidays and symbols—eggs, evergreen trees, rabbits, fertility rites, solar observances, and renamed pagan festivals—have origins outside Scripture. These are not neutral substitutes. The women of the Bible show us another way. They kept their households aligned with God's commands, taught their children His statutes, and honored His appointed times. And crucially, every feast they kept then still honors Christ now—not by erasing the feast, but by revealing its fulfillment. The High Holy Days were shadows in the Old Testament, but the body is Christ. He did not abolish them; He embodied them.

The Appointed Times of God — All Honor Christ

- **Sabbath (Day of Rest)**
  Then: A weekly sign of the covenant, commemorating creation and God's rest.
  Now: Christ is Lord of the Sabbath. Keeping the Sabbath honors Him as Redeemer, reminding us that there is a time to work and a time to rest.

  How to Keep it: Honor the Sabbath by ceasing from your own labor, setting the day apart for rest, worship, and remembrance of God as Creator. No working, Buying or selling, cooking, or housework. Relax and worship!

- **Passover (Pesach)**
  Then: Deliverance from Egypt through the blood of the lamb.
  Now: Christ is our Passover Lamb (1 Corinthians 5:7). His blood delivers from sin and death.

  How to Keep it: Honor Passover by coming together as a household or community to share the Passover meal, remembering deliverance through the blood and teaching the story of redemption to the next generation. The first day of Passover is a Sabbath, set apart for rest and worship, and today we honor Christ—the true Passover Lamb—by examining ourselves, breaking bread in remembrance, and rejoicing in the salvation He has secured. The meal consists of unleavened bread, bitter herb, red wine or grape juice, and lamb (although the unleavened bread is considered the body of Christ- the sacrificial lamb).

- **Unleavened Bread (Chag HaMatzot)**
  Then: Removal of leaven (sin) and separation from Egypt.
  Now: A call to walk in sincerity and truth, laying aside sin because Christ's sacrifice made holiness more accessible.

  How to Keep it: Honor Unleavened Bread by removing leaven from your home and examining your heart for sin, pride, and compromise. Walk in sincerity and truth, living a life purified by Christ's sacrifice and empowered toward holiness. It lasts seven days. Each day, eat unleavened bread. The first and last days are Sabbath days, no working on these days.

- **First Fruits (Yom HaBikkurim)**
  Then: The first harvest offered to God, guaranteeing what would follow.
  Now: Christ's resurrection—the first fruits of them that slept (1 Corinthians 15:20).

  How to Keep it: Honor First Fruits by thanking God for resurrection life and trusting Him for what is yet to come. Celebrate Christ's resurrection as the guarantee that all who belong to Him will also rise. This is the true 'Easter' minus the bunny rabbits and eggs.

- **Pentecost (Shavuot)**

  Then: Giving of the Law at Sinai; empowerment of a nation.

  Now: Giving of the Holy Spirit (Acts 2), writing the Law on the heart.

  How to Keep it: Honor Pentecost by coming together in holy assembly as a community, remembering the giving of the Law and celebrating God's covenant with His people. The Pentecost is a Sabbath, a holy convocation set apart for rest, worship, and rejoicing, and today it is honored by gathering together to celebrate the giving of the Holy Spirit and walking in obedience with God's law written on the heart.

  Blowing of Trumpets (Yom Teruah)

  Then: A call to awaken, repent, and prepare for judgment.

  Now: Points to the return of Christ, the resurrection, and the gathering of the saints.

  How to Keep it: Honor the Feast of Trumpets by coming together in holy assembly and literally blowing the shofar, sounding an alarm that calls God's people to awaken, repent, and prepare for His coming judgment and kingdom. It is a Sabbath, a day of rest and sacred gathering, reminding us today to live watchfully in expectation of Christ's return, the resurrection, and the gathering of the saints.

Day of Atonement (Yom Kippur)
Then: National cleansing through the high priest.
Now: Christ is our eternal High Priest (Hebrews 9), making final atonement once for all. A day of fasting.

How to Keep it: Honor the Day of Atonement through humility, repentance, fasting, and reconciliation with God and others. Honor Christ by trusting fully in His atoning work and walking in repentance and forgiveness. This is a high Sabbath day, no working.

- **Feast of Tabernacles (Sukkot)**
  Then: God dwelling with Israel in the wilderness.
  Now: Points to Christ dwelling among us (John 1:14) and the coming Kingdom where God tabernacles with humanity.

  How to Keep it: Honor Tabernacles by dwelling in temporary shelters—often through camping or building a booth—to remember Israel's journey in the wilderness and God's faithful provision. The first and last days of the feast are Sabbaths, set apart for holy rest, worship, and rejoicing before God.

- **The Last Great Day (Eighth Day / Shemini Atzeret)**
  Then: Completion and renewal beyond the feast cycle.
  Now: Foreshadows the final resurrection, judgment, and eternal life.

  How to Keep it: Honor the Eighth Day by gathering for sacred assembly and rest, recognizing it as a Sabbath that concludes the feast cycle. This day points to completion and renewal, directing our hope toward the final resurrection, judgment, and eternal life with God through Christ.

The New Moon

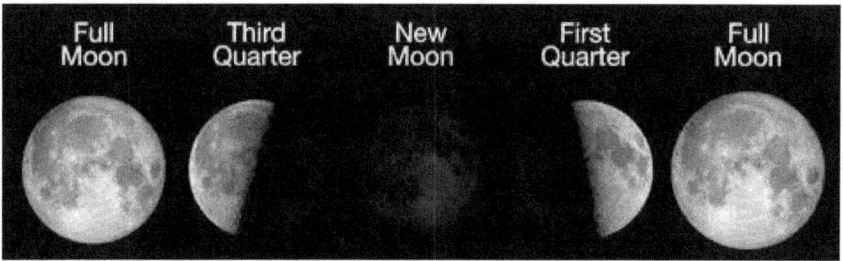

The New Moon is kept by recognizing the beginning of God's month (not the calendar month) through gathering, prayer, and remembrance that God orders time, seasons, and worship. Scripture teaches this plainly: *"He appointed the moon for seasons"* (Psalm 104:19), showing that God Himself established the moon as a timekeeper for His people. Honoring the New Moon helps the church body stay aligned with God's calendar rather than man-made systems, restoring unity, order, and covenant awareness in worship.

From Eve to the women who stood at the empty tomb, God's faithful daughters kept His commandments, guarded their households, and honored His appointed times. These feasts were never about ritual alone—they were about Christ then concealed and Christ now revealed. The question for women today is not whether tradition is popular, but whether obedience still matters. The women of the Bible answered that question with their lives.

Chapter 21: From Culture to Covenant

The women of the Bible did not drift through undefined relationships or casual intimacy. They courted with purpose and entered covenant through marriage. Their unions were intentional, family-centered, and rooted in responsibility before God. From Rebekah to Ruth, from Mary to Elizabeth, relationships were not about convenience or experimentation—they were about legacy. These women understood that intimacy carries consequence, and that love without covenant leaves women exposed. In contrast, much of modern culture encourages dating without direction, sex without vows, and emotional attachment without protection. Too often, women of faith are pressured to look like the world in order to be chosen by it—sharing beds without shared futures, giving bodies without security, and forming bonds without accountability. That was never God's design.

This is not condemnation—it is clarity. When we know better, we are called to do better. The women of Scripture planned their families through discipline, wisdom, and restraint. They did not treat children as accidents or inconveniences, nor did they outsource responsibility when choices led to consequences. They built households with foresight, not panic. Our past is not a prison sentence, but it *is* a teacher. Grace does not excuse disorder; it empowers transformation. The time has come for women of faith to rise again as queens, mothers, and wives, clothed in holiness, self-respect, and purpose—no longer shaped by the culture, but by the covenant.

About the Author

Karajah Yashar is a graduate of Rutgers University and serves as an author, publisher, teacher, and counselor with a clear mandate: to restore biblical understanding in a generation shaped more by tradition than truth. In 2016, he founded Passed Over Press (formerly Blackstone Publishing), an Orlando-based publishing house devoted exclusively to producing Scripture-centered books that honor the commandments of God and the testimony of Jesus Christ. Through his writing and teaching, Karajah focuses on biblical literacy, covenant identity, and practical holiness—calling readers back to the foundations laid out in Scripture rather than the shifting customs of modern religion.

Karajah wrote this book with the conviction that women are not peripheral to God's plan, but essential to it. He recognizes that as the Commonwealth of Israel is rebuilt under Jesus Christ—those once "aliens from the commonwealth of Israel" now restored through Him (Ephesians 2:12)—women will stand alongside men as builders, teachers, keepers of households, and carriers of covenant faith. This work honors the women of Scripture not as exceptions, but as patterns, reminding readers that restoration is communal and generational. For Karajah, reclaiming biblical womanhood is not about restriction, but about dignity, purpose, and alignment with God's original design for His people.

www.PassedOverPress.com
PassedOverPress@gmail.com

www.ingramcontent.com/pod-product-compliance
Lightning Source LLC
Chambersburg PA
CBHW071732120626
46550CB00002B/496